"In my 40 years of teaching math, I have worked with many children and young adults who found it confusing, frustrating, and frightening. This book offers exciting insights and applications which inspire learning, in addition to opening our eyes to God's majesty and power in creating this amazing world of ours."

> —Jane Ellis, Professor of Mathematics at Lake Tahoe Community College (retired, 2010)

• • •

"*Wonders In Our World* provides Christian educators a valuable resource and the confidence from which to thoughtfully bridge conversations and make connections between the physical and spiritual world. The book inspires young people to discover the glory of God which creation displays—to open their eyes anew to the Creator of all things."

> —Catherine Tippen- a specialist in Christian Curriculum Development (Dallas, TX)

• • •

"When reading *Wonders In Our World* I enjoyed seeing scientific facts explained clearly enough for non-scientists and children to understand. Why should the wonders of the world not be spiritually experienced? I live in a Retirement Community and look forward to sharing these wonders with my aging friends."

> —Bernice J. Dye, ARNP (nurse practitioner, retired)

• • •

"A remarkable unification of two lines of inquiry—Scripture and science—that leads the reader to a fuller comprehension of God's plan for ourselves and our world."

> —Jason Poznaks, Pastor to Children's Ministry, North Coast Calvary Chapel, Carlsbad, CA

Wonders In Our World

Insights from God's Two Books

Cheryl Touryan

Kenell Touryan

Lara Touryan-Whelan

Black Lake Press
TELL YOUR STORY
BLACKLAKEPRESS.COM

Wonders in our World: Insights from God's Two Books
Copyright © 2011
Cheryl Touryan, Kenell Touryan, Lara Touryan-Whelan

Editorial, interior, and cover design by Greg Smith

Published by Black Lake Press of Holland, Michigan.
Black Lake Press is a division of Black Lake Studio, LLC.
Direct inquiries to Black Lake Press at *www.blacklakepress.com.*

ISBN 978-0-9839602-3-2

contact the authors through their website:

www.wondersinourworld.blogspot.com

Dedicated to:

Troy Sarkis Whelan

And to all children who gaze in wonder at God's Creation.

"Why are you here on earth?
To behold."

—Anaxagoras (a pre-Socratic Athenian thinker)

Table of Contents

HOW DO I FOLLOW JESUS?

Comments on the Cover: The Golden Ratio, also called The Golden Number

The cover of this book includes five photographs (from top to bottom): a hurricane, a sunflower, a spiral galaxy, a chambered nautilus, a pinecone. Each of these is a picture of a spiral ranging in size from a few centimeters to millions of light-years across. But the amazing thing is that they all have the same mathematical configuration. This configuration or ratio is called the Golden Ratio and was most likely first calculated by Euclid around 300 B.C. It is a number or ratio that appears everywhere in nature from galaxy formations to the shapes of tiny sea creatures to the arrangements of petals on a flower. Its value is the number phi, which is 1.618033988.... Phi has no ending number and never repeats its pattern of numbers. In mathematics this is called an irrational number. This number was further defined by Leonardo de Pisas (also known as Fibonacci) in 1202 when he discovered what is known as the Fibonacci Series. This series of numbers is developed by adding together two sequential numbers to get a third number, with the first number in the sequence being 1, 1. It begins this way: 1, 1, 2, 3, 5, 8, 13, 21, 34,...etc. If we divide each number by the preceding number (2/1, 3/2, 5/3,...) the decimal results of these consecutive ratios will approach phi (1.618...) The consistent pattern displayed in all of these spirals is a 'wonder' in our world. The spiral is called a logarithmic (equiangular) spiral. It has the property that any line drawn from the center point of the spiral to any point on the perimeter always meets the spiral at the exact same angle. It is a direct dimensional relationship with phi.

This logarithmic spiral is also special because it fits nicely into the Golden Rectangle, whose sides are in the proportion of 1:1.62. The Golden Rectangle is often used in art and architecture, since it is a shape that is pleasing to the human eye and seems proportional and balanced. (This example was prepared by Luiz Real and is available on Wikimedia Commons.)

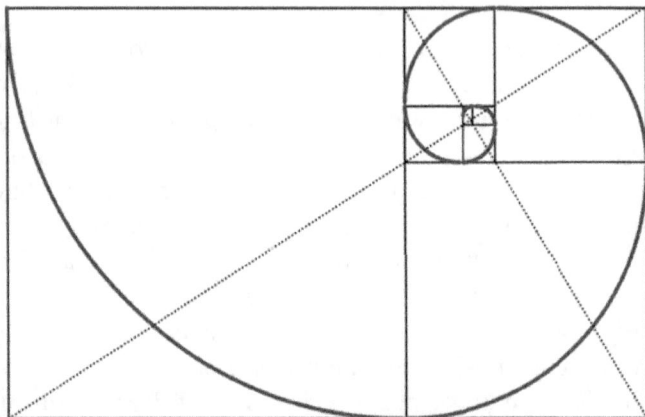

A close-up view of a sunflower or pinecone shows spirals going in both a clockwise and counterclockwise direction. The number of spirals shown in both directions are always consecutive numbers in the Fibonacci series and therefore, in the ratio of phi.

There are many more interesting features and uses of this amazing ratio, but most importantly, it shows the mysterious and amazing design detectable in nature. It is even more miraculous that we humans can understand something as abstract as a geometric formula and then relate the mathematics to physical phenomena in nature. God has given us minds that can understand these physical mysteries and comprehend the relationship between theory and the physical world.

As Eugene P. Wigner, Nobel Laureate in Physics, said, "The correspondence between mathematics and the physical world is a miracle which we cannot comprehend or even deserve" (Eugene P. Wigner, *Communications in Pure and Applied Mathematics*, vol. 13, No. 1, Feb. 1960, New York, John Wiles and Sons).

Preface

This book is the culmination of many years of interaction among the members of our family, as we have struggled with most of the issues included in these pages. My husband, Kenell, and I, wanted our children to grow up with a burning curiosity about the world around them as well as a deep commitment to the Christian faith. Since we have always believed that "all truth is God's truth" there was nothing to fear by asking questions, even very difficult question, and we encouraged our children to do just that, challenging them with questions they might not have thought of.

Kenell has been fascinated by science since childhood. He received his Ph.D. in Mechanical and Aerospace Engineering from Princeton University, with a minor in Physics. Since then his scientific career has spanned various specialties, with his last 20 years being spent in renewable energy technologies at the National Renewable Energy Laboratory in Colorado.

With a degree in Anthropology, Cheryl has also been drawn to the wonders that science reveals as well as the complexity and diversity of human culture and language. Together we have explored some of these wonders of nature and found that they consistently point us to a Creator God. Our hope is that these lessons will nurture that sense of wonder which comes naturally to children so that as they grow they might enjoy both the wonders of creation and the wonder of the Creator.

Today all our children are married and have children of their own. Two of our three children have Ph.D.'s in the sciences and two of their spouses also have Ph.D.'s. All members of our family are also deeply committed Christians, serving in their churches and beyond. Lara, our oldest daughter, has a Ph.D. in Material Science. She planted the seeds for this book when she organized a "Science Elective" for a ministry at her church, North Coast Calvary Chapel, in Carlsbad, California. Every summer the church has an outreach to all the neighborhood children called KidsGames (www.kidsgames.com). Hundreds of children show up, and one of the choices they have during their time at Kid's Games is to participate in the Science Elective. There Lara prepared the first lessons using some of the examples included here. Her lessons, combined with Kenell's life-long passion for apologetics and the integration of science and faith, have formed the core material.

Feeling that it was important to reach more children, including our grandchildren, with these important insights, my husband and I started to organize and further expand them. Our greatest joy would be for young people to acquire a love of science when working through this book, as well as an appreciation of the truth claims of the Christian faith. As has been said, "Metaphysical wonderment leads to worship and physical puzzlement leads to scientific investigation."

—Cheryl Touryan

Acknowledgements

We would like to thank Bernice Dye, wife of well-known physicist David Dye (recently deceased), who would not allow us to neglect this project and kept encouraging us to finish the book. She was also the first to proof the final copy. We needed her gentle nudging. We also want to thank Cathy Tippin, Jane Ellis-Touryan, as well as Joanne and Ted Finkler, who took the time to carefully proofread the book and offered numerous suggestions, corrections and additions. We have incorporated most of their contributions into the final version. Finally, we wish to thank Greg Smith of Black Lake Studio, who also encouraged us to publish this book and offered the practical help that turned a 'mountain' into a 'molehill.'

Special thanks goes to Michael Whelan, a geotechnical engineer, for writing the section entitled "Time According to the Rocks." We also thank Dr. Edward Davis, Professor of the History of Science at Messiah College, for allowing us to freely use his article on Robert Boyle (Robert Boyle's Religious Life, Attitudes, and Vocation) in our chapter on 'Doing My Best.'

Most of the artwork is original, crafted by Cheryl Touryan, using a combination of markers and computer-aided alterations. Other diagrams and photos are primarily from two sources: NASA's website and Wikimedia Commons. We appreciate the open source policy of both NASA and Wikimedia Commons, which made it possible to add visual input to our written copy.

Finally, we want to acknowledge a fellow traveler on this journey who is also passionate about seeing the wonder and purpose in God's creation, Dr. Charles Gordon of Tyler, Texas.

Introduction

The Two Revelations

God has given us two books, the Bible and His Creation, which is the natural world we live in. The Bible could be called Special Revelation because it is "God's Voice." We can use it to learn about his mind, his will, his character, his plans and his love. Nature, on the other hand, could be called General Revelation because it is open and evident to everyone on earth, no matter where they live or what their culture. In nature we see God's fingerprints, where we can understand something about his work, his person, his power and his intelligence. In the Bible we see God's heart and begin to understand his love for us and his purpose in creating us.

The Two Laws

Laws: There are also two types of laws. The Bible gives us moral laws, like "You shall not steal," and "You shall not tell lies." Nature tells us about God's physical laws, like the Law of Gravity, the Law of Electromagnetism and the Law of General Relativity. These laws are the same throughout the physical universe. When we fail to understand God's physical laws and break them, we pay the consequences. If we jump off a high deck, we suffer consequences like broken bones or a concussion. In the same way, when we break God's moral laws we reap the consequence of hardening our conscience, often lying to cover up our wrong, and if we don't turn back to God, developing a barrier in our relationship with him.

Science and the Christian faith (theology) are each ways of interpreting the data we have in front of us. Science is the means we use to interpret nature. Theology is the means we use to interpret the Scripture. An accepted definition of 'Science' proposed by the American Association for the Advancement of Science (AAAS) is: "Authentic Science is a way of knowing based upon testable descriptions of the world obtained through the human interpretation in natural categories of publicly observable and reproducible sense data, obtained by interaction with the natural world. (methods used: induction, deduction; abduction)."

On the next page is an illustration first proposed by the American Scientific Affiliation to help us better understand the relationship between God's first "speaking forth" (logos) in which he created the world and his second logos, where he spoke through the writing of men to bring forth the Bible.

God

Logos (CREATES)   **Logos (SPEAKS)**

Givens (Data)

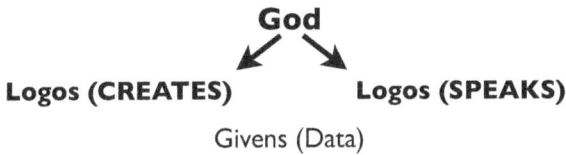

Nature	The Bible
Human Interpretation via Scientific Method	Human Interpretation via Biblical Interpretation Methods
Scientific Description	**Theological Description**
In order to Know Understand Control Develop Technology	In order to Know Understand Relate Serve
Concerned with Objects	**Concerned with Persons**
• Inquiry • Mechanism • Probability • Ask 'What' • Relationship to things • Evolution • Chance • Body/Brain • Animal • Machine • Temporal • Physical • Secular	• Commitment • Meaning • Purpose • Ask 'Why' • Relationship to persons • Creation • Divine Care • Soul/Mind • Human Being • Made in God's Image • Eternal • Spiritual • Sacred

TWO ASPECTS BUT ONLY ONE REALITY

In the column on the left the goal is to understand and control nature. On the right, the goal is to understand how God wants us to love and serve one another. The purpose of the scientific endeavor is to answer questions about how the 'heavens' work. The purpose of theology is to understand who God is and how he is at work among us. Galileo put it succinctly by saying, "The purpose of science is to tell us how the heavens go, and the purpose of Scripture is how to go to heaven." These are two aspects of the same Truth but one Reality.

Understanding this Book

This book has been organized around basic questions asked by almost everyone: Who is God? Who am I? What do I need to do to please God? They are first of all personal and theological questions. However, we believe that since God has spoken through his Two Books, we can also see similar principles in nature. Our desire is to help young people better understand themselves and their world, through a learning process that looks at "both sides of the coin," or two aspects of the same reality.

Each chapter is composed of four sections:

1. Insights from God's Book—the Bible

2. Insights from God's Book—the Physical World

3. Insights gained from trying to integrate God's Two Books

4. Hands-on fun with Science

Part I

Who Is God?

God is the Designer

*"What I have said, that will I bring about;
what I have planned, that will I do."*

Isaiah 46:11

When you walk around your house you see many things: furniture, computers, toys, TV's, dishes and washing machines for example. All of these objects were at one time an idea in someone's head. A thinking person had an idea, which he imagined and sketched out, worked on, supplemented with new ideas or improvements, and finally assembled, turning the idea into a reality. Today much of what we have is built by people, often at various locations but tied together by a plan. Everything begins with an idea and a plan. We call the person who had the initial idea the designer/inventor.

When we walk around outside, in nature, we can see the same process at work. In this case, God is the Designer and everything we see in nature comes from him. God is an artist and an engineer. He designs things of beauty like the sunset and the peacock's tail. He also designs things that work amazingly well like the water molecule, which is perfectly designed to fulfill thirty critical functions: for example, it is the only molecule that expands when it freezes and rises to the surface of bodies of water, allowing marine life to survive. Paul writes in Romans 1: 19-20 *"By taking a long and thoughtful look at what God has created, people have always been able to see what their eyes as such can't see: eternal power, for instance, and the mystery of his divine being."* (The Message)

In our secular society today people often say that everything we see in the natural world has come about through material forces and chance encounters, instead of design. They claim that there is no designer behind nature, no purpose, but everything just happened by chance over a very long period of time. To believe this claim takes more faith than believing that the universe was created by a designer, someone with intelligence and someone who created things for a purpose. John Locke, considered to be one of the most influential of the Enlightenment thinkers (1632-1704), said, "The visible marks of extraordinary wisdom and power appear so plainly in all the works of the creation, that a rational creature, who will but seriously reflect on them cannot miss the discovery of a Deity."

The Prophet Isaiah writes: *"Lift up your eyes and look to the heavens; Who created all these? He who brings out the starry host one by one, and calls them each by name. Because of his great power and mighty strength, not one of them is missing."* (Isaiah 40:26)

In response to Job's complaints about his unjust suffering, God showed Job his mighty power by asking him questions about the universe. *"Where were you when I laid the earth's foundation? Who marked off its dimensions? Who stretched a measuring line across it? Have you comprehended the vast expanses of the earth? Have you entered the storehouses of the snow or seen the storehouses of the hail, which I reserve for times of trouble? Can you bind the beautiful Pleiades? Can you loose the cords of Orion? Can you bring forth the constellations in their seasons? Do you know the laws of the heavens? Do you know when the mountain goats give birth? Do you*

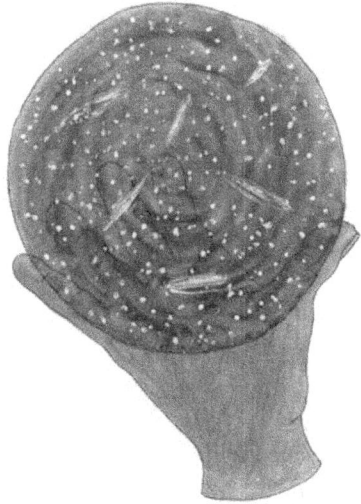

give the horse his strength or clothe his neck with a flowing mane."

Finally Job repented and humbly said, *"Surely I spoke of things I did not understand, things too wonderful for me to know."* (Job 38-42, portions) Although it takes faith to believe that God is the Designer, God has provided enough evidence in nature and in the Bible for us to intelligently accept him as Designer. It also takes faith to believe that the universe, the earth, and all life are a result of chance processes. This belief cannot be proven and goes against every natural human instinct. Faith in a God who is intelligent, powerful, and good gives us a purpose for living and a reason to praise him. *"Now faith is being sure of what we hope for and certain of what we do not see. This is what the ancients were commended for. By faith we understand that the universe was formed at God's command, so that what is seen was not made out of what was visible."* (Hebrews 11:1-2)

The Laws of Physics cannot explain how something can come from nothing. This is a mystery. These laws can only explain what happened at the very beginning of 'something.' Beyond this they cannot go. In the first book of the Bible, Genesis, we have an account of creation. This account is not meant to be a description of the science behind the beginnings of the cosmos, but a description of God's creative process in language that can be understood by people living in the pre-scientific age (4,000 years ago). Although it is not 'science' per se, it is by far the most 'rational' description of creation from among any of the 60+ creation stories among the world's cultures. The process fairly accurately follows what we now know happened 'in the beginning.' However, the creation account is primarily meant to introduce us to a God who is almighty and also personal, and who has created for a purpose —to have a relationship with his creatures.

God is the Creator

"In the beginning God created the heavens and the earth."

Genesis 1:1

From mankind's earliest days there is evidence that people wanted to understand the world they lived in. They often developed creation myths to explain the origins of their world. Many cultures included stories of a distant creator-god who created numerous lesser gods who then created and/or manipulated the physical world. The creation myths of these numerous cultures are far removed from anything science understands today about how the universe came about.

The people of Mesopotamia believed that in the beginning there was only freshwater (the god Apsu) and salt water (the goddess Tiamat). These two united to create the first gods and goddesses. Their offspring were very rowdy and fought often. Finally, Ea, the grandson of Apsu rose up against his grandfather and killed him. The goddess Tiamat, Ea's grandmother, was so angry she attacked him with eleven monsters. When she was finally killed, half of her body became the sky and the other half became the earth.

The Greeks had several stories about how the world came to be, but the most common involved the bird Nyx, who flew over nothingness. Nyx laid a golden egg and eventually Eros (love) hatched. The two half shells of the egg became the sky (Uranus) and the earth (Gaia). Eros caused them to fall in love and they produced many gods and goddesses. These offspring were always fighting and causing fear among their elders, so much so than one god, Kronus, swallowed his own children. His wife hid the youngest child so he wouldn't be swallowed. That child was Zeus. He eventually clashed with the older gods (the Titans) and after winning the battle, divided up the cosmos among the younger generation of gods: Poseidon ruled the sea, Hades ruled the underworld and Zeus ruled the heavens.

The ancient Egyptians believed in a god (Nu) who was "all," both male and female. Nu gave birth to Nut, who became the goddess of the sky (left), and Geb who was the earth god (left). They in turn gave birth to children like Osiris and Isis. Osiris was the god of the seasons and the earth, but he was killed by his brother, Seth, and in death, became god of the underworld. Isis was the sister and wife of Osiris. Her tears created the Nile River and she had a son, Horus, who guarded dead souls and protected the Pharaoh.

24

These creation myths are wonderful stories, but stand in stark contrast to the Biblical account of creation in their explanations of how the universe was actually formed. The Biblical account of creation is in line with what science today proposes as the process of creation, more so than any other creation account. Compare Genesis 1 and 2 to the creation accounts mentioned above, or to other creation mythologies.

[Genesis 1:1] In the beginning God created the heavens and the earth. ² *Now the earth was formless and empty, darkness was over the surface of the deep, and the Spirit of God was hovering over the waters.* ³ *And God said, "Let there be light," and there was light.* ⁴ *God saw that the light was good, and He separated the light from the darkness.* ⁵ *God called the light "day," and the darkness he called "night." And there was evening, and there was morning—the first day.*

⁶ *And God said, "Let there be an expanse between the waters to separate water from water."* ⁷ *So God made the expanse and separated the water under the expanse from the water above it. And it was so.* ⁸ *God called the expanse "sky." And there was evening, and there was morning—the second day.*

⁹ *And God said, "Let the water under the sky be gathered to one place, and let dry ground appear." And it was so.* ¹⁰ *God called the dry ground "land," and the gathered waters he called "seas." And God saw that it was good.* ¹¹ *Then God said, "Let the land produce vegetation: seed-bearing plants and trees on the land that bear fruit with seed in it, according to their various kinds." And it was so.* ¹² *The land produced vegetation: plants bearing seed according to their kinds and trees bearing fruit with seed in it according to their kinds. And God saw that it was good.* ¹³ *And*

there was evening, and there was morning—the third day.

[14] And God said, "Let there be lights in the expanse of the sky to separate the day from the night, and let them serve as signs to mark seasons and days and years, [15] and let them be lights in the expanse of the sky to give light on the earth." And it was so. [16] God made two great lights—the greater light to govern the day and the lesser light to govern the night. He also made the stars. [17] God set them in the expanse of the sky to give light on the earth, [18] to govern the day and the night, and to separate light from darkness. And God saw that it was good. [19] And there was evening, and there was morning—the fourth day.

[20] And God said, "Let the water teem with living creatures, and let birds fly above the earth across the expanse of the sky." [21] So God created the great creatures of the sea and every living and moving thing with which the water teems, according to their kinds, and every winged bird according to its kind. And God saw that it was good. [22] God blessed them and said, "Be fruitful and increase in number and fill the water in the seas, and let the birds increase on the earth." [23] And there was evening, and there was morning—the fifth day.

[24] And God said, "Let the land produce living creatures according to their kinds: livestock, creatures that move along the ground, and wild animals, each according to its kind." And it was so. [25] God made the wild animals according to their kinds, the livestock according to their kinds, and all the creatures that move along the ground according to their kinds. And God saw that it was good. [26] Then God said, "Let us make man in our image, in our likeness, and let them rule over the fish of the sea and the birds of the air, over the livestock, over all the earth, and over all the creatures that move along the ground."

[27] So God created man in his own image, in the image of God he created him; male and female he created them.

There are five important truths that we learn from the creation account in Genesis 1:

1. **God is one.** There are not many gods but only one God, all powerful, all seeing, all knowing, the creator of everything. The Jews were the first peoples to worship a single almighty God and began the first of the three monotheistic (one god) religions of the world—Judaism, Christianity and Islam.

2. **God is transcendent.** God is separate from his creation and not an extension of it. God created the world but is not a part of it. God created the sun, but he is not the sun. God created the animals, but he is not found in the animals. God created man in his image, but that does not imply that men and women are gods.

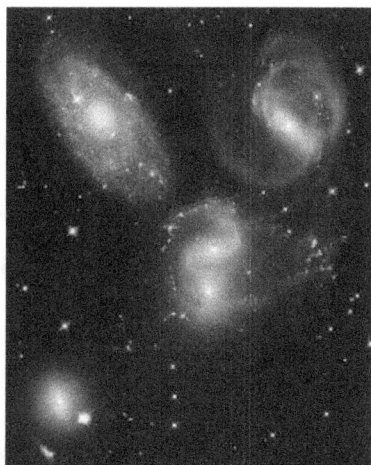

Stephan's Quintet: first identified galaxy group (NASA photo/Hubble Telescope)

3. **God created something out of 'nothing:'** Physically speaking, it is impossible to imagine something coming from nothing. And yet in Hebrews 11:3 by faith we understand that the universe was formed at God's command, *"so that what is seen was not made out of what was visible."* Space and time

Swan Nebula: a bubbling ocean of hydrogen, oxygen & sulphur (NASA photo/ Hubble Telescope)

have not existed forever, but were created by God. (see Titus 1:2) This is also unique to the Judeo-Christian understanding of God. He spoke and things came into existence. Notice how many times the words 'God said' appear in Genesis 1.

4. **God created something good**: Many religions believe that the physical world is bad and people must not take pleasure in creation. Many Eastern religions believe, in fact, that the physical world is only an illusion, something that is not real but exists only in our imagination. The Bible, however, tells us that God declared his creation good and took pleasure in it. He then gave mankind the job of taking care of this good creation.

5. **God created for the purpose of relationship**. Although God is not an extension of his creation, he does continue to sustain it. He also desires to have an intimate relationship with each of us. Beginning in Genesis 1 through 3, we can see that God is very interested in what is happening on earth, especially in people's hearts and minds, and

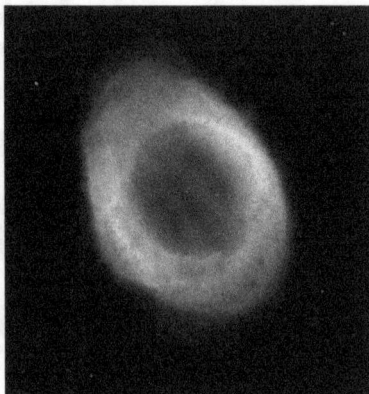

M57 Ring Nebula, also called "Eye of God" *(NASA photo/ Hubble Telescope)*

wants to have a relationship with the people he created. Adam and Eve heard God walking in the Garden of Eden and because they sinned, they ran and hid. But God called to Adam, *"Where are you?"* (Genesis 3:8-9) God has chosen to make himself knowable through his creation. You might say he is playing hide and seek, for he says that anyone who really seeks him, will find him. (Jeremiah 29:13) Anyone who truly wants to know God can know him, for Apostle

Paul says that *"since the creation of the world God's invisible qualities—his eternal power and divine nature—have been clearly seen; being understood from what has been made, so that men are without excuse."* (Romans 1:20)

Science Facts: Understand Origins

When we study nature (the physical world), we come up with two basic questions: 1) How did the universe come into existence and how did life begin? 2) How does everything work? The first question has to do with what scientists call the problem of origins. The second has to do with laws that govern the physical world, both animate (living) and inanimate (non-living). To answer these questions, we observe in nature three active agents: laws that are regular and predictable, laws that are based on chance events, and finally, what looks like design by an intelligent agent. Many scientists who do not believe in God, talk about 'apparent design' and yet reject the idea of a Designer, trying to explain all phenomena through natural laws only (regular laws or chance happenings).

However, when it comes to explaining how all of creation came into existence, science faces problems it cannot answer through natural laws alone. For example, there is overwhelming evidence that the universe came into existence 13.7 billion years ago through a Big Bang; the visible universe came into existence from 'nothing.' Physics can describe how the universe began by using physical laws that take us to an exceedingly short time called the Plank time, 10-43 seconds (that is 0.00000...a total of 43 zeros).1. But science has nothing to say about how everything came from nothing. What is also interesting to note is that after the initial Big Bang, for about 380,000 years (as measured on earth), the universe was completely dark due to the very high gravitational forces which trapped even light waves and kept them from escaping (similar to a black hole).

About 380,000 years after the Big Bang, the gravitational force weakened as the baby universe continued expanding, allowing light to escape, and there was a tremendous burst of light (just as Gen. 1:3 says, *"And God said, "Let there be light…"*) The echoes of this 'burst' we hear today in what is known as cosmic background radiation (CBR).

In addition, scientists have now discovered that the universe and all of nature are so precisely tuned such that a very slight change in the laws that govern nature would make physical life as we know it impossible. For example, if the force of gravity on the surface of the earth were only 10% stronger, the atmosphere will contain poisonous gases like methane and ammonia and animal life would not be possible. If gravity were 10% weaker, the water on earth would eventually turn into vapor (as on Mars) and again life would cease to exist. There are at least 120 such parameters all of which have to be so precisely tuned that the only logical explanation would be that the universe/nature has been designed by a super-intelligence.

As the famous astronomer Fred Hoyle has said, the odds of all of this fine tuning happening only by chance is equivalent to a tornado going through a junkyard with the outcome being a fully assembled Boeing 747 airplane. The precise ordering of the universe seems to anticipate the emergence of conscious life on a single planet like our earth that can observe it. Scientists call this the Anthropic Principle. Nobel Laureate Freeman Dyson has said, *"As we look into the universe and identify the many accidents of physics and astronomy that have worked together to our benefit, it almost seems as if the universe must in some sense have known that we were coming"* (Reference1). This is why we find that what the Bible says about a personal God creating the universe and all of life makes much more sense than denying his existence.

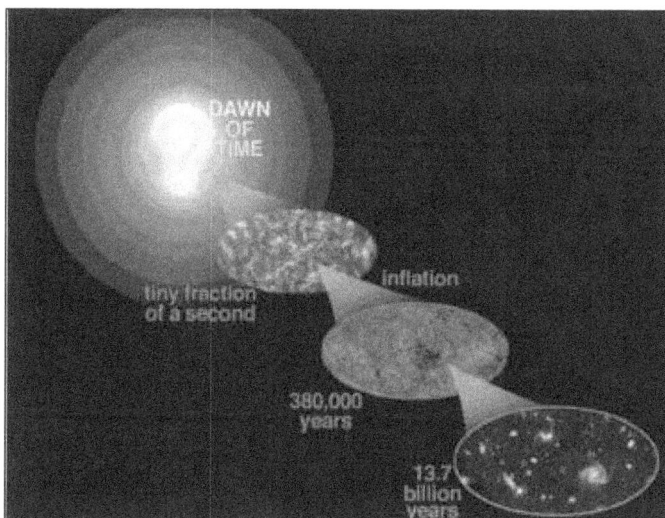

An illustration of the creation of the universe: from Big Bang to Galaxy Formation. (Illustration courtesy of USDOE)

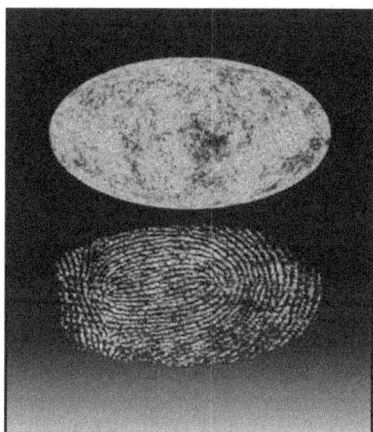

Early Universe: map of cosmic microwave background radiation (COBE) and the map overlaid with a representation of God's fingerprint. The fingerprint implies the work of a designer. (*Courtesy of the Jet Propulsion Laboratory, NASA*) The various colors on the map represent tiny temperature deviations of one part in 100,000 that gave birth to all the galaxies in the universe, as the universe continued expanding. This extreme precision indicates a designer, symbolized by God's fingerprint in the creation of the universe.

Fun with Science

BLACK HOLES: Learn more about Black holes from the experts: www.scienceface.org

COSMOLOGY and THE UNIVERSE: www.nasa.gov

This website has information on both the universe and NASA space flights. Check out the collection of amazing photos of space from the Hubble Telescope on "Image of the Day." The "News" and "Media" sections will probably be most interesting to explore.

Google **"NASA for Kids"** to find some wonderful sites for kids of all ages. Be sure to find the "NASA for Kids" section. Another site has been put together by the Goddard Space Flight Center, under the auspices of NASA. There is a portion of the website dedicated to younger children called **"StarChild."** On this website you can find out how much you would weigh on another planet in our Solar System or how old you would be. You can plan your own space mission and play video games about space travel.

"Imagine the Universe" has been developed by NASA, for teens age 14 and older. On the "Imagine the Universe" website there is a lot of age appropriate information on Dark Energy, Dark Matter, Black Holes, Quasars, Galaxies, The Milky Way and much more.

HAVE FUN!

God is Spirit

"God is Spirit and his worshipers must worship in spirit and truth."

John 4:24

One day when Jesus was traveling with his disciples, they passed through an area called Samaria. The people who lived there were snubbed by the Jewish people, who considered the Samaritans 'half-breeds', people who mixed with pagans. But Jesus gave some of his most important teachings to a Samaritan woman, someone with whom his Jewish disciples would not even dare to speak.

Jesus asked this woman for a drink of water and from that request the discussion turned to living water. Jesus had a wonderful way of using physical objects to teach spiritual truths. As he discussed this 'living water' with the woman, she saw that he was not an ordinary man, but a prophet. *"So you are a prophet! Well, tell me this: Our ancestors worshiped God at this mountain, but you Jews insist that Jerusalem is the only place for worship, right?"*

Jesus replied, *"Believe me, woman, the time is coming when you Samaritans will worship the Father neither here at this mountain nor*

there in Jerusalem…It's who you are and the way you live that count before God. Your worship must engage your spirit in the pursuit of truth. That's the kind of people the Father is out looking for: those who are simply and honestly themselves before him in their worship. God is sheer being itself—Spirit. Those who worship him must do it out of their very being, their spirits, their true selves, in adoration." (John 4:20-24, The Message)

What does it mean that God is sheer being-Spirit? Spirit is non-material, something not physical but from another dimension. Spirit also means that there is emotion, will, desire and passion involved. To say 'God is Spirit' means that God is not visible, not physical, is infinite, exists in another reality, and is greater and more powerful than the physical. It also means that God is personal: he exhibits emotions like love, anger, tenderness and joy. He is not just a 'force.' As created beings who have been given a spirit we live in two realities: the natural and the super-natural. Jesus came to help us understand the nature of spiritual reality.

When Adam and Eve disobeyed God in the Garden of Eden, they broke their close connection to God. This was the beginning of their death, first spiritual and much later physical. God has made us with the ability to connect to Him in our spirit. The creation account in Genesis 1 says that God placed a 'life-force' (*nephesh*) in the animals he created. When he created Adam however, he breathed into Adam the *"neshamah"* or 'spirit-force' to distinguish humans from the animal world. The Fall in the Garden of Eden broke the spirit-force connection to God and only Christ can restore the connection through his death on the cross. When we trust in the work of Christ and begin to seek God, our spirit is able to perceive a new dimension, a super-natural dimension, and we begin to understand things differently.

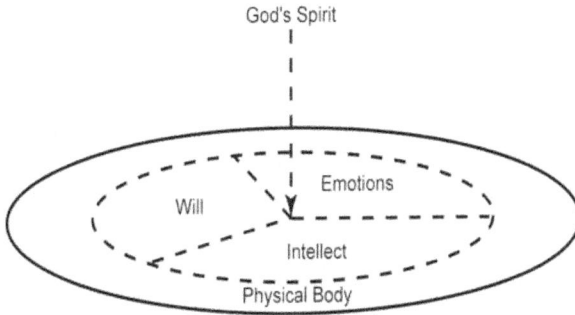

This diagram helps us to visualize this difficult concept. We are like the flat, two-dimensional circle, our body being the outermost circle which other people who are also circles, see. Inside the circle we have a soul, a *nephesh* in Hebrew or *"psyche"* in Greek, which consists of our will, emotions and mind. But when our spirit (*neshamah* in Hebrew or *pneuma* in Greek) is restored, we can enter another dimension and that dimension (God's Spirit) can also enter us and change us. *"It is written: The first man Adam became a living being, the last Adam (Jesus) a life-giving spirit. The spiritual did not come first, but the natural, and after that the spiritual. The first man was of the dust of the earth, the second man from heaven. As was the earthy man, so are those who are of the earth; and as is the man from heaven, so also are those who are of heaven. And just as we have borne the likeness of the earthy man, so shall we bear the likeness of the man from heaven."* (1 Corinthians 15:45-49)

Science Facts: Understanding Dimensionality

Higher Dimensions

A famous scientist by the name of Hermann Minkowski proposed that our universe is made up of four dimensions and not just the three that we are aware of, i.e. length, width and height. Minkowski added a fourth dimension called 'time', which Albert Einstein later used to formulate his Theory of General Relativity. As human beings, we can only visualize three-dimensions. But four-dimensions are necessary for us to have a stable universe that can exist over a long period of time. In other words, we live in a four-dimensional space-time continuum.

There are four forces that govern the universe. They are as follows: 1) the electromagnetic force between charged particles; 2) the gravitational force between masses; 3) the strong force which exists in the nucleus and binds the protons and neutrons together; and 4) the electro-weak force which also operates inside the nucleus and is a million times weaker than the strong force. During the past fifteen years several mathematicians/physicists like Dr. Edward Witten (Reference 2) realized that in order to fully explain the interaction of these four forces in a unified manner, scientists needed to go to eleven-dimensions, of which seven are hidden. These dimensions existed for a billionth of a billionth of a second after the Big Bang, but then seven-dimensions folded into a very tiny space, called the Plank distance, which is 0.00000000000000000000000000000001 (10-33) centimeters.

Currently, scientists have no way of proving the existence of these 'invisible' dimensions, except by constructing models such as the String Theory Model first proposed by Witten. Several astrophysicists who do not support belief in an intelligent designer, have put forth a new theory called the Multiverse Theory. Briefly, the theory proposes that there were many, many universes that started with a Big Bang and one of them happened to have the physical laws needed for life as we know it to emerge in our particular universe. In this manner, they try to avoid the need for a creator and attribute everything to probability and chance events.

It requires very large accelerators on earth to generate energies like those that existed at the beginning of the universe. In fact, the **Large Hadron Collider** recently built in Europe, may be able to find the existence of these super-dimensions proposed by Witten, when it starts operating at full power. This collider sends two very powerful proton beams toward each other, traveling at close to the speed of light (300,000 km/sec). When these beams collide they generate energies close to the energies that existed three minutes after the Big Bang explosion, at the creation of the universe approximately 13.7 billion years ago.

Insights from God's Two Books

Today all scientists accept these extra dimensions by 'faith', or as a theoretical model, because there is no empirical evidence for these dimensions. So when scientists who do not believe in a creator or in the supernatural (God, angels, heaven, hell, etc), dismiss the existence of an invisible, spiritual dimension, they are being hypocritical because they themselves put faith in invisible dimensions and unknowable multiverses. In fact, according to the laws of physics, which would be different in each of the multiverses, there can be no communication between these various universes, which makes belief in them even more speculative. When Christians speak of another dimension or reality, they are accepting by faith a 'reality' that cannot be seen or understood, just as some scientists do when they believe in dimensions that cannot be experimented on, experienced or understood. Unlike the Multiverse Theory, which allows for no communication between the universes, Christians can communicate with the spiritual dimension through prayer. God, as the one who created the universe with all its dimensions, can also be very close to us in our 4-dimensional existence. The Apostle Paul said, *"The God who made the world and everything in it is the Lord of heaven and earth and does not live in temples built by hands. ..From one man he made every nation of men, that they should inhabit the whole earth...God did this so that men would seek him and perhaps reach out for him and find him, though he is not far from each one of us. For in him we live and move and have our being"* (Acts 17: 24-28).

To help us better understand the spiritual dimensions we are talking about we can use the example of a torus. A torus (see illustration) is a surface of revolution generated by revolving a circle in three dimensional space about an axis in the same plane as the circle. A doughnut, for example, is a torus. Below, on the first plane you can see two circles. They seem to have no connection at all. But when you add the torus (seen in the bottom illustration) you can see that the two circles are all a part of a whole. Adding a third dimension helps us see the connection. One of the purposes of this book is to help you see the connection between science and Christianity. At first they seem to be unrelated—two entirely different subjects. But if God is behind both, then they are part of a wonderful whole and relate to one through the third or spiritual dimension.

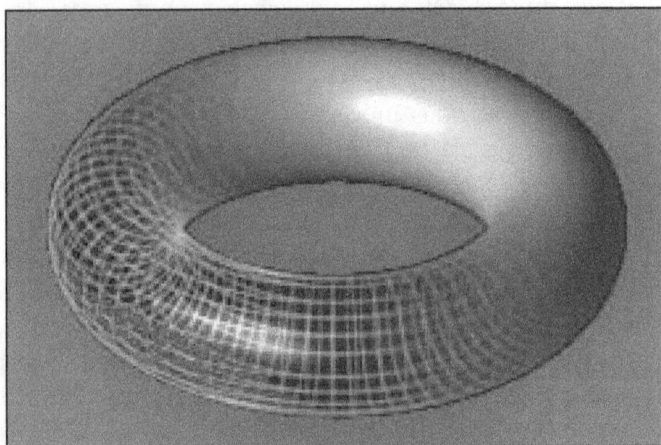

A Torus *(Illustration from Wikimedia Commons)*

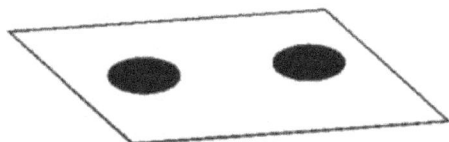

Two Dimensions

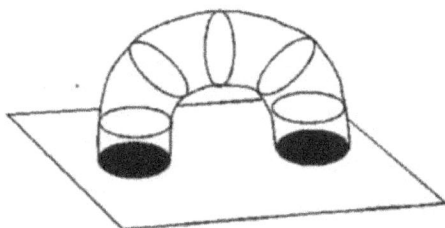

Three Dimensions

Fun with Science

We know that a dimension is a measure of spatial extent: length, width and height. A length measured in inches, feet, miles, centimeters, meters or kilometers is called one-dimensional space. An area measured in square inches, etc., is called a space of two-dimensions. A volume measure in cubic inches etc, is called a three-dimensional space. Another way of putting it, a line has only length, an area has length and width whereas a volume has length, width and height.

How much freedom would you have if you only existed in a space of one-dimension? Draw a line and try to move on it! All you can do is move back and forth! Not much freedom, is it? Now pretend you are two-dimensional being that can only move on a flat surface. Now you can go back and forth, and sidewise—a little more freedom. Now move around in three dimensions, which is how you normally move. You can go back and forth, sidewise, and up and down. That gives you a lot more freedom!

In the universe, we have one more dimension called time; thus, we live in four-dimensional space-time continuum, which we cannot visualize but can express mathematically. In order to grasp a higher dimension like the one God exists in, try the following exercise:

Cut out two human figures using a sheet of paper. Draw a heart in each paper figure. These figures will now be two dimensional. Put them on a table and bring them close to each other. Pretend you are one of the figures and your friend, the other. What is the closest you can come to your friend when you cannot go up and down? Can you see the *insides of your friend* (the heart) without moving up and down? Now imagine a third 'figure', let's say God, who lives in three-dimensions and CAN go up and down. Can He see your or your friend's heart? If he moves down towards your heart, how close can he come to you? He can almost touch your heart from above, can't he, something you cannot do to your friend, or your friend to you? If you use this analogy, you will understand how God can know your heart and can be closer to you than any other human being!

The illustration below helps us understand the difference between two and three dimensions. The squares are two-dimensional sheets of paper. On three of the square sheets of paper, there is a circle, which is the two-dimensional representation of a sphere intersecting the paper at that point. From the paper's point of view, there is simply a circle in view. Imagine that you are looking at the lower illustration (the spheres) from the side. You will see length, width and height—three dimensions. From the three-dimensional perspective, you see a sphere intersecting a flat plane (paper), and we can see both the paper and the entire sphere (Reference 3).

2-dimensional view (squares): length and width

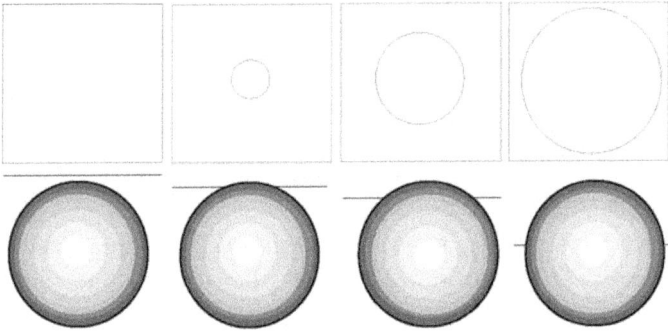

3-dimensional view (spheres): length, width and height

God is Eternal

"This is what the high and lofty One says, he who lives forever,
whose name is holy."
Isaiah 57:15

Probably the earliest written story in the world is *The Epic of Gilgamesh*. It is a mythological story of a man-god who lived and ruled in the area of today's Iraq. Gilgamesh had many adventures but in the end, the most important part of the story is his search for immortality. He wanted to live forever.

In the Garden of Eden there were two important trees: the tree of life and the tree of the knowledge of good and evil. Adam and Eve ate from the second tree—and, *"Became like God knowing good and evil." God then said, "He (Adam and Eve) must not be allowed to reach out his hand and take also from the tree of life and eat and live forever…So God placed on the east side of the Garden of Eden cherubim and a flaming sword flashing back and forth to guard the way to the tree of life."* (Genesis 3:23-24) In the Biblical story God builds a barrier to protect the tree of life and people are denied eternal life because of the sin of disobedience and lack of trust in God.

People have been searching for eternal life for as long as we know. *"God has set eternity in the hearts of men; yet they cannot fathom what God has done from beginning to end."* (Eccl. 3:11) This means that God, who is eternal, put the desire for things eternal, for eternal life, in the hearts of the people he created.

What does it mean to be eternal? It is very difficult to understand eternity. It is something that has no beginning and no end. On the other hand, the universe including planet Earth had a beginning, is continuing to exist, and some day will come to an end. (Psalm 102:25-26, *"It will wear out like a garment"*). It is impossible for us to imagine anything other than living in time. We are born, live a certain length of time, and then die. However, through the tool of mathematics, we can get a small glimpse of what living outside of time might be like.

There is a story in the book of Exodus about Moses and the children of Israel. God wanted to help his chosen people, the Israelites, who were suffering as slaves in Egypt. He chose a man named Moses to lead his people to freedom. But Moses was afraid that the Israelites would reject him and think he was crazy when he told them to gather up their things and walk out of Egypt. *"Moses said to God, "Suppose I go to the Israelites and say to them The God of your fathers has sent me to you and they ask me, What is his name? Then what shall I tell them? God said to Moses, "I*

am who I am. This is what you are to say to the Israelites: I AM has sent me to you." (Exodus 3:13-14)

"I AM" is an interesting name. It indicates that the person exists—period! He exists in the past, he exists in the present, he exists in the future—he is eternal. That is one of the first things God wanted his people to know. He also tells us this same thing at the end of the Bible. *"I am the Alpha and the Omega,"* says the Lord God, *"who is, and who was, and who is to come, the Almighty."* (Revelation 1:20)

God is eternal because he exists outside of time. In fact, God created time (2 Timothy 1:9 and Titus 1:2) when he created the universe. When he communicates with us, he tries to help us understand this difficult truth by explaining it like this: *"With the Lord a day is like a thousand years, and a thousand years are like a day."* (2 Peter 3:8)

So when people are seeking immortality, they really are seeking God, which is why he put the desire for eternity in our hearts. He wants us to seek him because he is also seeking us.

Science Facts: Understanding Time

When we mention the word 'time', the first thing that comes to mind is how the hours go by followed by days and nights, weeks, months and years. The reason we do this is because of the biological clock that God has put in each one of us. This clock is identified as the circadian rhythm of living entities. The name is based on the Latin word "circa" which means 'around' and "diem" which means 'day' and it is roughly a 24-hour cycle in the processes of living entities of all kinds, including plants, animals, and even bacteria. It is primarily based on the daily cycle of light and darkness.

In fact, time in the physical world has a direction determined by the **Second Law of Thermodynamics.** This laws states that in a closed system all energy and motion in the universe proceeds from an orderly state to a disorderly state, giving direction to time from the past to the present. This law does not allow for time to go backwards. If we take the universe as a whole, time is like an arrow moving from an ordered state at creation towards a disordered state, which eventually in the distant future, will degrade to a level where there can be no activity of any kind. Scientists call this final state a "cold, lifeless bath," which will be the "ultimate death of the universe."

And yet time can also be described as another dimension, added to our three dimensions of space (length, height and width) in the space-time continuum of the universe. Our hours and days are measured by the rate at which earth rotates around its axis (1000 miles per hour), and our months and years are measured by its orbit around the sun (30 km/sec).

In fact there is even more to the way we measure time than this. The solar system itself rotates around the Milky Way at 230 km/sec and the Milky Way moves at 600 km/sec relative to other galaxies. In other words, the earth is a real spaceship hurtling through space at enormous speed.

Time, therefore, is relative and depends on your location in space and your movement relative to the speed of light which is approximately 300,000 km/sec (in a vacuum).

According to the Laws of Relativity that Einstein first formulated, and which have been experimentally verified, if we move at speeds close to the speed of light (300,000 km/sec), time slows down. Imagine twin brothers or sisters. One stays on earth and the other travels near the speed of light in a spaceship. The one on earth will get old, whereas the one traveling near the speed of light will remain young! The same phenomena is true in a gravitational field. For example, if you were able to hover in a spaceship over a large black hole which has the strongest gravitation pull of anything in the universe, one year for you will be equivalent to millions of years on earth!

Insights from God's Two Books

The book of Genesis, chapter 1, points to two time categories. The first is the time frame within which God created the heavens and the earth, measured from the human perspective in billions of years. What we see as billions of years in the creation process, from God's perspective could have been a short time because of the stretching of space and time. Thus what humans see as billions of years would be equivalent to six days from God's perspective as recorded in chapter 1 of Genesis. The second time frame starts after Adam is created, when mankind becomes aware of biological/historical time. Once Adam was created, God began to work within the human time frame. That is one reason the Bible begins Adam's genealogy from the time he was created and does not include the history before that time, the creation of heaven and earth.

To this day Jewish people use a different calendar and count their years from the creation of Adam. For example, year 2010 A.D. for us is the year 5771 in the Jewish calendar. Many Orthodox Jews as well as most Christians in science do not interpret the six 'days' of creation as 24-hour days, for reasons described in the previous section on 'Understanding Time.'

Time According to the Rocks

Even the rocks you find around you tell a story of God's purpose over long lengths of time! While God works in our lives at the time scale of our human perception (hours, days, years), His work and will span much longer timeframes than that. As discussed in the section on Science Facts (above), he has created a world for us that appears to be BILLIONS of years old. The evidence for this is all around—the very rocks at our feet tell a story that spans amazing lengths of time!

Geologists have established three basic categories of rocks, each of which represents a different method of formation. IGNEOUS rocks are formed deep below the Earth's surface, starting as molten rock which then crystallizes and becomes solid. Much of the **IGNEOUS** rock that you typically find (such as granite) crystallized deep in the earth millions of years ago, and gradually became exposed at the surface after a long period of erosion, uplifting, or a combination of both. Find a piece of granite. It took millions of years for that piece of rock to melt, crystallize, and then to be exposed at the surface! There's no other way to form this kind of rock. This rock demonstrates that God's creative process has spanned millions of years!

Another rock type is **SEDIMENTARY.** This kind of rock is formed by the slow accumulation of sediment—sand, gravel, silts or clays that are eroded from the land and deposited in rivers, lakes, and seas. When enough sediment accumulates, and enough time passes, the layers of sand, gravel, etc. slowly compress and cement together, forming **SEDIMENTARY** rock. In the end, it tends to look like a layer cake, as you're seeing the individual layers of material as flat bands in the rock. The walls of the Grand Canyon are a spectacular example. Think of sedimentary rock that you've seen with your eyes or in pictures —it takes tens of thousands, even hundreds of thousands of years to create this kind of rock! There's no other way to do it!

And think of this—sometimes you'll see the layers folded, or faulted, disrupting the perfect "layer cake" appearance of the rock. That's the result of the earth's movements over time, through earthquakes, land movement, and similar processes. It folds the rock, or cracks it, or shifts it, changing the appearance of the layered rock. To us, with our mortal perspective of time, the earth's movements are practically imperceptible (except during the occasional drama of an earthquake, where one small part of the earth moves, maybe, several feet). But folded sedimentary rocks show us that this nearly imperceptible movement has been going on for such a long time, it's folded and faulted the rock itself, sometimes on a huge scale. Some entire MOUNTAIN RANGES are made of spectacularly folded layers of sedimentary rock. Again, the rock tells the story; God's creation spans millions of years.

The third class of rock is METAMORPHIC. The term comes from the word "metamorphosis"— to change—(like the caterpillar turns into a butterfly). Now, imagine a mass of IGNEOUS or SEDIMENTARY rock gets buried DEEPLY within the earth, and in so doing not only gets exposed to incredible PRESSURES, but also gets HEATED up to great temperatures. Under these conditions, when enough time passes, the rock types go through their own 'metamorphosis', becoming this new, third type of rock, with its own unique appearance and properties (but still with some faint resemblances to its previous form). You now have METAMORPHIC rocks. Common examples are schist, or gneiss. Generally it's made of undulating stripes with a crystalline appearance. Imagine all the time that was needed to produce igneous or sedimentary rocks, now adding an additional, spectacularly long period of time for this metamorphosis to occur! (and yet MORE time to expose the new rock at the earth's surface, where you can see it). Once again, the rocks tell the story—God has made us an Earth that has developed over many millions of years—there's no other way to make these rocks! What a profound thought! What incalculable power this God of ours demonstrates. He has existed over time spans so long we cannot even imagine them, yet we can hold the results of his work, stones and rocks, in our hands. When you see a rock, think of God... and time... and His unbelievable power and love.

Fun with Science

1. The globe is divided into 24 time zones, one hour apart. Do you know which time zone you live in? If you needed to make a call to Tokyo (or Sydney or Moscow) around noon their time, when would you need to make the call according to your time? Go to www.worldtimezones.com Find out how time zones are determined using lines of longitude. Compare your 'time' to the 'time' of other locations in the world. Where does time start its countdown? What is GMT?

2. Start with the time unit 'second' and list the units of time going up to longer and longer time units. Then start with the 'second' again and list the time units of shorter periods of time.

   Example: second   second

                   minute   millisecond (10^{-3})
                   :   :
                   etc.   etc.

   What is the longest period of time called?
   What is the shortest period of time called?

3. If a light-year is the distance light travels in 1 year and the speed of light is 300,000 kilometers/second, how many kilometers will a light-year be? What would that be in miles (1 mile = 1.6 km)?

Science Trivia: Do you know how the company "Google" got its name? What is a google?

The Number Googol *(Illustration by Hidro Yot, Wikimedia Commons)*

Answer: The term 'googol' is a mathematical term, 1 followed by 100 zero's (10^{100}). Basically it is a very, very large number, a number larger than anyone can imagine. However, it is not infinity. A 'googolplex' is 10 to the power of googol. When Larry Page and Sergey Brin founded Google, they had a vision of connecting a huge number of separate bits of information, so using the word 'googol' would be appropriate. However, they misspelled it and now Google is a word known around the world as a company that is able to connect a googol of information. A 'googol' is similar to 'time' in that it is a concept we cannot grasp except through mathematics.

God is Three in One—Trinity

"Anyone who has seen me (Jesus) has seen the Father. Believe me when I say that I am in the Father and the Father is in me...I will ask the Father and he will send you another Counselor to be with you forever... I will not leave you as orphans; I will come to you."

John 14:9, 16, 18

Probably the hardest thing to understand about God is how he can be one and three at the same time. Although the word 'trinity' is not found in the Bible, the doctrine of the trinity has been foundational to Christian belief since the 2nd century. It was then that a church father, Tertullian, first used the word to describe the way God is revealed in Scripture. He along with other church leaders tried to understand the puzzling way God is presented as God the Father, God the Son and God the Holy Spirit. Does this mean that there are three Gods? Yet Christianity's origins were in Judaism, which has a very strong belief in one God. A famous passage that Jews use even today is from Deuteronomy 6:4 called the Shma'a Israel. *"Hear, O Israel: The Lord our God, the Lord is one."*

The problem for these early Christians was how to reconcile the 'One God" with the three revelations or names that are given in the Bible. The three persons were present at the creation of the universe when God (*Elohim*) said, *"Let us make man..."* The word 'Elohim' in Hebrew is plural, implying 'one in unity' not 'indivisible one.' The three persons are critical to the story of redemption, or our salvation through Christ on the cross. This is summarized in the first chapter of Ephesians. Redemption was begun by the Father (verses 4 and 5) and put into place or accomplished by Christ (verse 7) and sealed or made sure by the Holy Spirit (verses 13 and 14)

The Trinity is defined as consisting of three distinct persons who share one divine essence. They are co-equal and co-eternal and all share the same glory and honor. The Trinity is three distinct persons, not just one person changing roles, so to speak, according to the situation. That would be like a man who is a son, and a father and a husband. He has three different roles according to his different relationships but is essentially one person. The theological term for this view is 'modalism', which is not consistent with traditional Christian teaching.

In Matthew 3:16-17 when Jesus was baptized by John the Baptist, it says, *"As soon as **Jesus** was baptized he went up out of the water. At that moment heaven was opened, and he saw the **Spirit of God** descending like a dove and lighting on him. And a **voice from heaven** said, "This is my son, whom I love; with him I am well pleased."* Here we see all three persons present at the same time. Jesus is referred to as God in Colossians 2:9 *"For in Christ all the fullness of the Deity lives in bodily form."* The Holy Spirit is referred to as God in Acts 5:3-4, when Peter accused Ananias and Sapphira of lying about the money they gave to the church. *"Ananias, how is it that Satan has so filled your heart that you have lied to the Holy Spirit... You have not lied to men but to God."*

The Trinity is impossible for humans to fully comprehend, but it does give us a beautiful illustration of complete unity and love among beings, which is the 'heart of God' and what he wants for all of us. God as Father, Son, and Holy Spirit have perfect love and harmony

among themselves, not seeking power over the others, but in everything submitting to each other. *"Christ Jesus, who being in very nature God, did not consider equality with God something to be grasped but made himself nothing, taking the very nature of a servant."* (Phil. 2:5). The Father calls us into this relationship, Jesus Christ paid the price for our acceptance and is constantly praying to the Father for us, and the Holy Spirit is at work in our daily lives and in the world, to do the Father's will and bring honor to the Father and Son. Isn't it amazing that we are called to be a part of this eternally loving family, the Trinity?

Science Facts: Understanding Diversity in Unity

There are many examples in nature of what may be called diversity in unity. A fruit tree can serve as an illustration of diversity in unity. Imagine an apple tree. It is composed of roots, branches, leaves and fruit. Inside the fruit, the apple, there is a seed that has everything required to produce another apple tree, if put in the ground and watered. The tree and the apple and the seed are each very different but they all share the same genetic code, DNA, in each of their cell nuclei. So in a way, you could say they share the same 'essence' or genetic structure but have very different functions and outward manifestations.

Many phenomena in nature occur in groups of three. Here are three examples that demonstrate this.

1. One of the best known 'triplets' is the so-called triple point of many substances under certain pressure and temperatures conditions. The triple point of water is the best known example. At near zero degrees centigrade and under very low pressures (0.006 atmospheres) water exists simultaneously as ice, liquid and vapor. It is the same substance, H_2O, but in three different phases.

This example of the triple point of water can help us, in a limited way, visualize the concept of the Trinity, three in one.

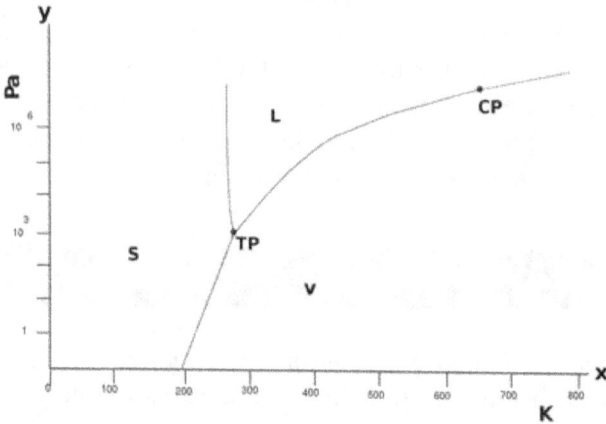

Water Phase Diagram
Y = pressure; X = temperature; S = solid;
L = Liquid; V = Vapor; CP = Critical point;
TP = Triple point
(Diagram by Eurico Zimbres, Wikimedia

2. The second 'triple' phenomenon in nature is that of the atom. All atoms are made up of three elementary particles: electrons, protons and neutrons. Other than the hydrogen atom which has only two particles, one electron and one proton, all other atomic structures are composed of three particles.

3. One of the most fundamental particles in nature is the quark, which makes up the protons and neutrons. Quarks never occur singly. They make up protons and neutrons in groups of three. There are 'up' quarks (u) and down quarks (d), that come in three colors, as shown in the diagram

below (Reference3, page 12).

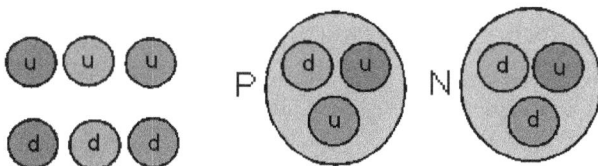

They belong to the same class of elementary particles, namely quarks, but each has a different function.

P = proton; N = neutron

One last example of a well-known triplet is the equilateral triangle which has three equal sides where each side touches the other two, creating a very rigid structure. If you notice, all metallic structures, such as bridges, radio/TV towers, etc. are constructed using triangles.

Insights from God's Two Books

All the parallels discussed under the Science Facts represent but a weak and inadequate picture of the mysterious concept of the one-triune God, but could be of some help to begin to grasp the significance and importance of the concept.

Among primitive cultures the most common belief in regards to the supernatural is the belief in many gods— polytheism. These gods can help or hurt humans and must be worshipped and given gifts to pacify them. A more advanced concept is seen in pantheism, the belief that all that is in the universe is god. The word *'pan'* in Greek means 'all' and *'theos'* means god. So pantheists believe that everything in the universe is god. This god is an all-encompassing impersonal being and everything that exists is a part of god.

The highest level of belief in the supernatural is the belief in a single, personal God who created heaven and earth. The religions that teach belief in One God are called monotheistic (*"mono"* = one; *"theos"* = god in Greek). The most complex and inscrutable view of God is the Christian belief in a Triune God; three persons, one essence. This is a concept so difficult to grasp by the human mind that it could only have been revealed by God himself. It is almost impossible to visualize or comprehend such a concept. The most we can do as thinking, rational beings is to approximate the concept by looking at parallels in nature.

Fun with Science

In every living cell there exists the organism's genetic code or DNA. The DNA is a huge information data base (think of a library with thousands of reference books) that has all the information needed for the organism to make every unique but necessary part of the whole. How does DNA, which is identical in every organism's cell nucleus, make so many different things, like bones, skin, or blood in humans? Remember that the smallest living unit is our body is the cell. These cells are made up of proteins which form the basis of all life and are synthesized in the cytoplasm through a process called Gene Expression. The key player in this process is the RNA polymerase (ribonucleic acid), which itself is a large protein complex. There are three types of RNA:

1. mRNA (messenger RNA) that transcribes or rewrites parts of the DNA, depending on which protein is needed. Proteins are made up of amino acids.

2. rRNA (ribosomal RNA) serves as a template that accepts the tRNA that carries or attaches to the amino acids.

3. tRNA (transfer RNA) are small RNA molecules that carry

a specific amino acid. It binds to the mRNA codon* thus determining which amino acid should be added to the protein chain.

You could think of it like this: Mary goes to the library and writes down the information needed to make a certain chain. Mary carries this information to Ray, who then takes the information and gets everything ready for the chain to be formed. Trudy has all the parts but does not know how to assemble them. She comes to Ray who guides her in the assembly, and when the work is done, she folds the newly made chain in a specific way to make it more compact and able to fit into the exact space needed.

These three RNAs all work together in an integrated complexity to turn the information in the DNA into a beautiful, 3-D protein. Thousands of these proteins then participate in virtually every process in a cell as essential parts of an organism. (Reference 5)

* codon—3 bases on a mRNA molecule that code for a specific amino acid base (A,C,G,T, the 4 letters in the DNA molecule chain).

For a 3 ½ minute video animation of how gene expression works in the cell, go to www.signatureinthecell.com

For a more detailed presentation of how the DNA/RNA works, you can order a DVD from Discovery Institute (Seattle, WA) entitled, **"Unlocking the Mystery of Life."** There is a section of the DVD which features a detailed computer-generated animation of exactly how the cellular transcription process works.

God is Sovereign

"The Sovereign Lord comes with power and his arm rules for him."
Isaiah 40:10

A sovereign is someone who rules in a monarchy, usually a king or queen. In the case of God, He is sovereign over his kingdom, which is a heavenly kingdom. Jesus said, "My kingdom is not of this world." (John 18:36) When we pray the Lord's Prayer as instructed by Jesus, we are asking that God would bring his kingdom rule to earth. "Thy kingdom come, thy will be done, on earth as it is in heaven." Christians desire and pray that God would rule the earth in righteousness, justice and mercy. Many people ask the question, "How can God be sovereign and all-powerful and let so much pain and suffering and injustice continue on earth?" It is one of the hardest questions Christians must face.

When God made people, he desired a relationship with us since He made us in his image. He did not want us to be mere puppets, doing his will because he was pulling the strings. He wanted us to freely choose to love him because he loves us. Mankind chose to break that relationship, beginning in the Garden of Eden, because we did not trust in God's goodness but instead wanted to make our own choices based on what we felt was 'good' for us. That is why God called the forbidden tree the Tree of the Knowledge of Good and Evil. In order to have choices, there needs to be something to choose. That is why God has allowed Satan to continue having power on earth. People can choose between trusting in God's love or following Satan's temptations. There is a battle going on for the souls of men and women, boys and girls.

When people long ago chose to reject God, he did not give up on them, but developed a plan whereby all people could come back into a relationship with him. The price of accomplishing this plan was huge. God himself (in Jesus Christ) suffered all the pain and injustice in the world, and paid the price for it, so that mankind can freely choose him again and be in a restored relationship. God does not force us to choose him but draws us to himself in love. We only need to give up our pride and willfulness and submit to God.

This is a paradox: where two seemingly opposing truths (God's sovereignty and man's free will) exist in harmony. How can God be sovereign and yet mankind have the power to choose? God gives everyone on earth clues or evidence of his power and character. These can be seen in nature (Rom.1:20), in a person's conscience (Romans 2:14-15) and also in the witness of his people (2 Corinthians 3:2,3). In everyday life, everyone acts as if he or she has free will. You make a choice to study and you reap the consequence of getting a good grade. We are created to make choices and our choices count. In fact, it is a bit scary to think how important our choices can be.

The Bible seems to indicate, however, that when a person continues to reject God there comes a time when it is impossible to go back and accept his love. (Hebrews 6:4-6) This would mean that by making wrong choices, it becomes harder or even impossible to make right choices. We can never tell when this time is in another person's life, but we do know that for everyone, free will ends at

death. We must make a choice before dying. *"Man is destined to die once, and after that to face judgment."* (Hebrews 9:27)

So what can we say about the suffering in the world? God is at work in the world but he is limited by the choices people make. He is building his kingdom and we are invited to be a part of it. Jesus referred to the kingdom of heaven in many of his parables. It is a 'secret' kingdom, seemingly small and weak in the world's eyes, but one day, this heavenly kingdom will rule when Christ returns as sovereign Lord. We can be an active part of God's Kingdom even today through our obedience to his Word.

Science Facts: Dealing with Paradoxes in Science

A paradox is two observations, each of which is correct by itself, but when put together seem to contradict each other or cannot be explained.

In the 18th century, Isaac Newton and Gottfried Leibnitz formulated the classical laws of mechanics, whereby the motions of matter, subject to gravitational forces, could be predicted precisely, once initial conditions are determined. This and other formulations such as electromagnetism by Clark Maxwell, led to the belief that nature obeys pre-set laws that can be used to predict any and all future events. In other words, that nature is predestined to behave in a certain way or is 'deterministic.'

However, in the early 20th century, when the laws of quantum mechanics were formulated to describe the behavior of elementary particles, such as electrons, protons, neutrons, and photons, something unexpected happened! It was discovered that at the elementary particle level *everything* about the behavior of these particles could not be determined and one had to use probability rules to locate particles. In fact, Werner Heisenberg showed that it is impossible to determine both the position and velocity of electrons at the same time, with equal precision. It almost seemed like the electrons, photons and other elementary particles had 'free will' and were behaving in a way that could not be predicted.

All these interesting scientific findings show us that even nature, macroscopic phenomena such as the behavior of large bodies, obey deterministic laws, but the fundamental particles that make up these large bodies behave very differently, in a very indeterminate and apparently contradictory manner.

Insights from God's Two Books

Thus, the seeming conflict between God's sovereignty and his ability to control everything in creation versus an individual's free will and ability to act independently, presents us with a paradox. But we see that same paradox *in the physical world!* In fact, all of the most fundamental phenomena in nature, especially at the microscopic level, appear as paradoxes. As you know by now, a paradox represents two truths, each of which is correct *by itself,* but seem to contradict each other when put *together.*

Therefore, we can confidently say that science is unable to completely explain the nature of physical phenomena, but accepts physical reality *as it appears to us.* So we can accept, as a paradox, the reality of a sovereign God who has made creatures like us who do have free will as a paradox, even if we cannot fully grasp how the two realities work in our lives.

Illustration of God Outside of Time

This diagram illustrates the one-dimensional linear time humans experience, starting with a beginning or birth (B), flowing in one direction (P = present time) and ending with death (D). God who exists outside time, 'sitting' on top of this hemisphere, sees all of existence, or the flow of time at once. In fact, he can interact with our linear time through many time-dimensions as illustrated above. [U = beginning of universe; E = end of universe]

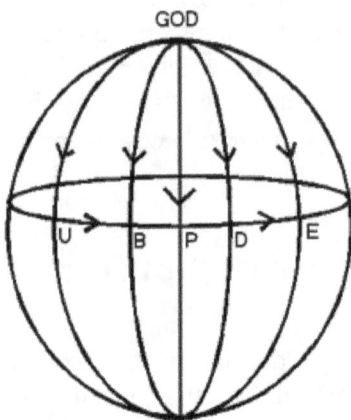

GOD

(see Reference 4, based on diagram by Dr. Hugh Ross, from *Beyond the Cosmos*, page. 57, used with permission)

Fun with Science

Quantum mechanics is a more recently developed field of science. In many ways it contradicts the laws of classical mechanics because of the influence of the uncertainty principle first explained by Heisenberg. Quantum mechanics studies the behavior of the tiniest particles in the universe, or more scientifically, elementary particles which are the building blocks of all matter and energy.

An interesting experiment called the 'double-slit experiment' has been done by scientists studying quantum mechanics, in which they record the behavior of light. Light as mentioned above is both particle and wave. When focused light, like laser light, travels through a partition with two slits in it, you would expect that two lines of light would appear on the wall opposite the double-slit partition. In fact, when light passes through one slit, it does appear as a lighted strip on the far wall.

Double-slit experiment

A stream of light through one slit behaves like particles or photons.

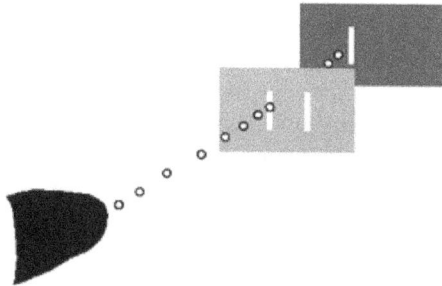

However, when light (photons) passes through two parallel slits, the pattern appearing on the far wall is not two strips but a series of strips, such as would appear if light were made up of waves. The waves interfere with each other causing light to be strongest where the waves intersect.

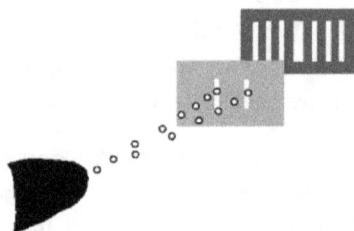

A stream of light sent through both slits behaves like waves.

This experiment is a clear demonstration of the truth that light is both particles and waves. This is a paradox, which only recently science has begun to explain. This paradox applies to all elementary particles such as electrons, protons, and neutrons. It is called the particle-wave duality.

To see this experiment and for a great explanation, go to www.YouTube.com and search for 'double slit experiment video.' It is an excellent animation featuring Dr. Quantum, explaining the experiment (uploaded by ReptilianShapeshifte). There are several other videos on YouTube that also explain this issue of particle-wave duality.

God is Love / God is Just

"God is love. Whoever lives in love lives in God, and God in him."

1 John 4:16

"God is just: He will pay back trouble to those who trouble you."

1 Thessalonians 1:6

How can God be both loving and just? This is a very hard question and many people are never able to answer it. If God is loving why doesn't he execute justice on all the bad people? If he is loving and lets people join him in heaven, even many bad people, how can he be just? If he is just and requires that all his commandments be obeyed, how can he love anyone, because we all commit sin?

We can understand something about this paradox by studying the Jewish Day of Atonement, which was first described in the Old Testament. This is the most important day in the Jewish religion. When God gave his laws to the Israelites, he included laws about how the High Priest was to bring an annual sacrifice to the temple for the sins of the people. This was the most important sacrifice of the year because through this sacrifice the people would be clean in God's eyes and would have another year of God's blessing. The High Priest was to dress in special garments and first make a sacrifice for himself and his family. Then two goats were brought to him, and he was to cast lots to see which goat would die and which would be released. *"He will offer the goat on which the lot falls to God as an Absolution Offering. The goat on which the lot falls will be sent out into the wilderness to make atonement."* Then the priest was instructed to kill the selected goat and sprinkle its blood in the

Holy of Holies as well as on the large altar before the Tent of Meeting.

"When Aaron finished making atonement for the Holy of Holies, the Tent of Meeting, and the Altar, he will bring up the live goat, lay both hands on the live goat's head, and confess all the iniquities of the People of Israel, all their acts of rebellion, all their sins. He will put all the sins on the goat's head and send it off into the wilderness, led out by a man standing by and ready. The goat will carry all their iniquities to an empty wasteland; the man will let him loose out there in the wilderness" (Leviticus 16, *The Message*).

In this picture we can see both God's justice, by requiring the death (blood) of an animal, and God's love. After the first goat was killed, the second symbolically took on all the sins of the people and was taken far away, showing that when our sins are paid for in blood, God does not count them against us any more. *"God does not treat us as our sins deserve or repay us according to our iniquities. For as high as the heavens are above the earth, so great is his love for those who fear him; as far as the east is from the west, so far has he removed our transgressions from us."* Psalm 103:11,12

Science Facts: Understand Solar Radiation

The sun radiates both life-giving and harmful rays. These rays are part of the electromagnetic spectrum. At one end (high wave length) is the infrared and the visible rays which provide heat and light and sustain life. At the other end are ultraviolet (UV) radiation and x-rays, both of which are harmful to life. In addition, the sun is the source of what is known as the solar wind, composed of charged particles such as electrons and protons, which reach the earth at very high speed, and unless filtered, would destroy life on earth.

The ozone layer around the earth is one filter that absorbs most of the UV radiation such that only a small amount reaches the surface of the earth and that is what causes us to tan. Too much of this UV radiation will cause skin cancer.

The earth also has a magnetic field that extends from the north pole to the south pole and is called a dipole field. This magnetic field acts as a filter by trapping the high energy electrons and protons that come from the sun as part of the solar wind. In fact, the aurora borealis is a visible example of how these electrons and protons interact in the upper atmosphere, ionize the air, and create the beautiful colors we see.

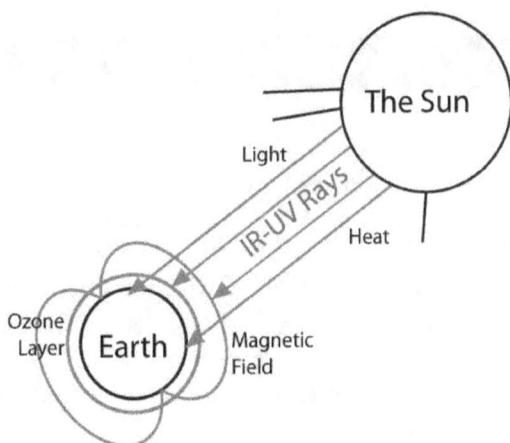

One of our nearest neighbors, Planet Mars, which is very similar to the earth in size, has neither an ozone shield nor strong magnetic field and thus is unable to stop the harmful UV radiation and the solar wind from reaching its surface. Even though several NASA probes have landed on Mars since 1972 and tested its soil, they have found no life on the planet. The most recent Mars rovers were called Spirit and Opportunity.

The reasons for lack of life on Mars is: (1) it does not have an ozone layer, so UV radiation freely reaches the surface and inhibits the formation of large organic molecules essential for life; and (2) it has a very weak magnetic field which is unable to stop the solar wind hence the bombardment of electrons and protons on the planet's surface which are harmful to organic life.

Insights from God's Two Books

The cross plays a central role in the Christian faith. Jesus Christ inextricably tied God's love for the world to his own death on the cross (John 3:14) and referred to the cross time and time again, often to the consternation of his closest followers (Matt 16:21-23)

The Apostle Paul made the cross his central theme in his first letter to the church in Corinth (I Cor. 1:23-24) and again in Galatians 2:20 and Galatians 6:14. Throughout the twenty centuries after the death of Christ, the cross has become the very symbol of Christian faith, adorning churches, used to bless congregations, practiced as a hand symbol of sincerity and honor, and hung on necklaces. Armenians, with their tradition of being the first nation to adopt Christianity, have almost no decoration that does not include the symbol of the cross, with its ultimate expression found in the ubiquitous *khatchkar* (crosses carved in stone with intricate designs), which are strewn throughout the countryside of Armenia.

In his first letter to the Corinthians, the Apostle Paul describes the cross, as the unique method used by God to provide salvation to mankind, which was foolishness in the eyes of the contemporary Greek intellectuals and a sign of weakness for the Jews.

And yet, one finds a depth of wisdom in God's choice of the cross that surpasses the greatest intellectual achievements of mankind! As with so many of the methods the Creator has used in reestablishing the broken relationship with his creatures, the cross bears witness to God's genius in dealing with an intractable dilemma: How to reconcile God's wrath against evil with his love for his fallen creatures. The cross has become the unique and only means whereby God's righteousness and love can be properly reconciled. To better appreciate the importance of the cross in bringing Creator and creature together we resort to the following illustration from nature.

The sun/earth radiation phenomena described in Science Facts has an uncanny application as an illustration of the relationship between God and man. Just as the sun generates both life-giving radiation (IR and visible) and life-destroying radiation (UV, electrons, protons, x-rays), the God of the Bible by his very nature is described as Holy God, who `radiates' rays of life and death, grace and judgment. The Bible describes God as he "who alone is immortal and who lives in unapproachable light" (I Tim. 6:16) As with the sun, the rays of life represent his love and mercy. The rays of death, on the other hand, represent his wrath toward sin, and his righteousness that demands punishment for evil. Man in his fallen, sinful state is subject to God's righteous judgment. Just as in the case of the sun and earth system, God chose the cross of Jesus Christ to operate as an ozone layer or a magnetic field to filter out his anger against sin and human unrighteousness but also to allow his rays of love and life to go through and reach human beings, giving them abundant life. God does this by offering his son, Jesus

Christ, as a ransom for sin. He was crucified on the cross and was made sin for us. Through his death, Christ absorbs God's rays of wrath. What filters through the cross, however, is his love and mercy. Anyone who stands behind the cross of Jesus, sees not God's judgment but rather his love and mercy. All the deadly rays have stopped at the cross. Christ's death absorbs God's punishment for sin. This is why Jesus cried on the cross, *"My God, my God, why have you forsaken me?"* (Matt. 27:46) However, when we take our place behind the cross we enjoy only his love and mercy.

At a first glance, the cross, a Roman `gallows' and an instrument of torture, seems foolish and weak. And yet, its simplicity belies the depth of God's wisdom, where he uses the deadly instrument to restore the broken relationship, initiated by man's disobedience and rebellion against God. He does this without compromising his sense of justice, or sacrificing his love for you and me.

See illustration below (Reference 5).

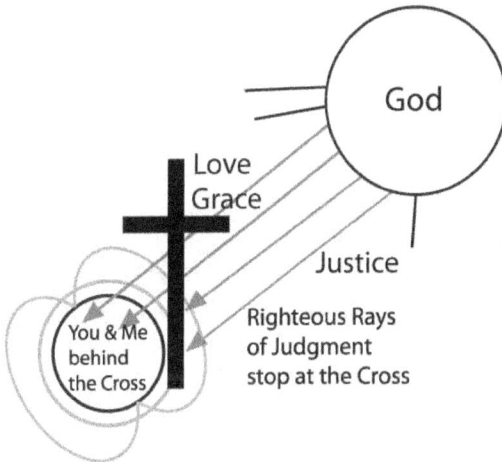

Fun with Science

As you have learned from the above discussion, our sun gives off both life-giving rays (light and heat) as well as dangerous rays such as ultraviolet radiation (UV). Excessive exposure to UV radiation can be destructive to life. UV rays are energetic and can breakdown organic chains such as proteins, kill living cells, and produce skin cancer when the skin has not been properly protected.

Fortunately, there is a protective layer in the stratosphere, called the ozone layer, which filters out most of the deadly UV radiation, allowing the life-giving rays of light and heat to reach the surface of the earth. Ozone is a gas that is made up of three oxygen atoms which have the unique property of acting as a filter in the stratosphere. It can also be used to kill microbes in water, purifying it.

For some fun experiments, we can learn how filters like ozone work by experimenting with optical filters that allow only certain wavelengths of light to go through, while stopping other wavelengths.

Try this:

✓ Take a colored glass, red, blue or green, and shine a flashlight through the glass onto a white sheet of paper and observe the color that falls on the sheet of paper. What do you think is happening? Each colored glass will only allow its own wavelength to pass through, and will stop all the other colors. Thus the ozone layer becomes an optical filter holding back the UV rays but allowing the rest of visible and IR rays to go through.

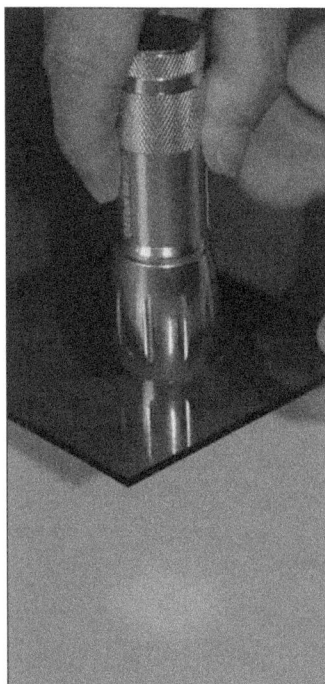

✓ Take a red sheet of paper and hold a red glass filter over it and look at the red sheet through the red filter. What color do you see? (In photo at left, both the white sheet and the red sheet of paper look the same.) Why is this happening?

How does this remind us of Isaiah 1:18 *"Though your sins are like scarlet, they shall be as white as snow; though they are red as crimson, they shall be like wool."* (NIV)

There are many other experiments you can do with filters and light. The following websites offer many science experiment kits and equipment for further study of light.

- www.sci-toys.com
- www.spectrumscientifics.com
- www.scientificsonline.com (Edmund Scientific's)
- www.hubbardscientific.com
- www.stevespangler.com

God is Light

"God is light; in him there is no darkness at all."

1 John 1:5

From the beginning of the Bible until the end, God is identified with Light. At the beginning of creation *"God said, "Let there be light and there was light. And God separated the light from the darkness."* (Genesis 1:3) God's Word is powerful enough to bring forth light. Light gives us the ability to perceive the visible universe and also brings the possibility for life to exist, for without light there can be no life.

But there is also an invisible world, the spiritual world, where God's Word brings forth light. The Prophet Isaiah said, *"The people walking in darkness have seen a great light; on those living in the land of the shadow of death light has dawned."* (Isaiah 9:2) This was a prophecy about the coming of Jesus Christ. A few verses later it is written, *"For to us a child is born, to us a son is given, ...and he will be called Wonderful counselor, Mighty God, Everlasting Father, Prince of Peace."* (Isaiah 9:6) When Christ entered our world he came to open our eyes so that we could see the reality of God's Kingdom. People did not know who God was or what God expected of them, so Jesus came to earth and became one of us, so that we could begin to understand the Light of God.

This is explained in the first chapter of the Gospel of John. *"In the beginning was the Word, and the Word was with God and the Word was God. He (Jesus) was with God in the beginning. Through him all things were made; without him nothing was made that has been made. In him was life, and that life was the light of men. The light shines in the darkness but the darkness has not understood it...*

The Word became flesh and lived for a while among us. We have seen his glory, the glory of the one and only Son, who came from the Father, full of grace and truth." (John 1:1-5, 14)

Jesus came to help people understand God. We have a hard time understanding that there could be a God who would love us enough to die for us. We usually think that we must 'do' something to be loved by God. Or we think that although God may love us, he surely could not love those really bad guys over there. Or sometimes people think that God does not love anybody because he allows so many bad things to happen. Jesus, by coming to us in the form of a human being, was able to communicate with us about these difficult concepts. He came to 'shed light' on the nature of God, so that we are better able to trust and love Him.

However, there are those who choose to live in the dark even though Jesus has shown them the light. Jesus said, *"This is the verdict: Light has come into the world but men loved darkness instead of light because their deeds were evil. Everyone who does evil hates the light and will not come into the light for fear that his deeds will be exposed."* (John 3:19-20)

"This, in essence, is the message we heard from Christ and are passing on to you: God is light, pure light; there's not a trace of darkness in him." (1 John 1:5, The Message) When we finally get to heaven to live with Him for eternity, we will no longer need the physical light he created, because God himself will be our light. In the last book of the Bible, there is a description of God's heavenly city where it says, *"The city does not need the sun or the moon to shine on it for the glory of God gives it light and the Lamb is its lamp. The nations will walk by its light."* (Revelation 21:23)

Science Facts: Understanding Light

Light behaves sometimes as waves and at other times as particles called photons. This is a paradox in nature. How can light be both waves and particles at the same time? This paradox presents a seemingly contradictory situation that nonetheless has been shown to be true. In fact, everything at the atomic level presents a paradox. As waves, light is part of what we call the electromagnetic (EM) spectrum. This spectrum or range of values for electromagnetic waves goes from very long waves measured in kilometers (radio waves) to very short rays, which are called gamma rays (a billionth of a centimeter). Our bodies are sensitive to different kinds of waves in nature. One type of wave is called a sound or acoustic wave which we are able to hear, and the other is called radiation waves which we are aware of through our bodies (heat as infrared radiation) and with our eyes (light as visible radiation).

The electromagnetic spectrum describes the range of electromagnetic waves placed in order of increasing frequency. At one end of the spectrum are radio waves, which have a very low frequency and long wavelength. At the other end of the spectrum are high-frequency (short wavelength) gamma rays. All electromagnetic waves travel at the same speed—the speed of light. They differ in the amount of energy they transfer, called electromagnetic radiation. Lower-frequency waves like radio waves emit less electromagnetic radiation than do higher-frequency rays like gamma rays.

Photons are one of the most fundamental particles in nature. They have no mass and consist only of energy. As mentioned above, the EM spectrum has a huge range of values of which light is only a tiny part. For example, the universe would be glowing bright, without any darkness, if our eyes were sensitive to the whole EM spectrum (i.e. infrared, UV, x-ray, gamma rays, etc.). Since they are not, we can only see the visible portion of these photons through our eyes, over a dark background (the night sky).

Light travels at a constant speed of 300,000 km/sec in a vacuum. Nothing exceeds the speed of light; therefore it is an absolute constant in nature. One more characteristic of radiation, including light, is that it carries huge amounts of information from one place to another. It is our best means of communication (radios, TV, internet, etc.). Radiation in general, and light in particular, brings us information from celestial objects including the moon, planets, the sun, the stars and galaxies at the very end of our universe. By studying the EM spectrum of these celestial objects, using an instrument called a spectrometer, we can learn what stars and galaxies are made of, even those that are millions of light-years away. A light-year is the distance it takes light to travel in one year at the speed of 300,000 km/sec. which is equivalent to billions of miles. With all these characteristics, light becomes an essential part of our existence, both as the source of all life through the photosynthetic process used by all green plants, and also as a source of information about the cosmos and all that is in it.

Insights from God's Two Books

In Genesis the first recorded words of God are: *"Let there be light."* Light and life are closely connected. The photosynthetic process used by plants converts light (plus water and carbon dioxide) into food which is essential for our existence. Light also enables us to see the world around us.

Jesus calls himself the Light of the World three times and is referred to as the Light seven times in the New Testament. The reason Christ called himself the Light of the World is because he came to give us eternal life and to open our eyes to distinguish good from evil. The Gospel of John says, "Christ came as light into the world to remove darkness," and darkness is identified with evil. There are striking parallels between the characteristics of light discussed above and how Jesus is the Light of the World. Here are the parallels between physical light and Christ:

1. Just as light has a **dual nature,** so Jesus Christ is both God and man. Just as it is hard to describe light as consisting of waves and particles at the same time, so it is impossible to understand how Christ can be both man and also God. (Mark 4:37-40)

2. Just as photons represent the most **fundamental particles** in nature, Jesus Christ is the visible image of the invisible God; all things were created by him and he is before all things. (Colossians 1:15-17)

3. Just as light is the **absolute constant** in nature, Jesus Christ is our ultimate standard, and our goal is to conform to his image (Ephesians 4:13; Rom. 8:29)

4. Just as light makes a difference between **life and death,** Jesus is our very source of life, both physical and spiritual. *"He who has seen the son has life."* (1 John 1:12)

5. Just as the **universe is filled** with photons (of all wave lengths, from radio waves to gamma waves), Jesus

Christ fills the universe. *"The Son......sustains all things by his powerful word"* (Hebrews 1:3) and in Acts 17:28 we read, *"In him we live, and move, and have our being."*

6. Just as light **carries information** by its frequency and amplitude, so Christ is God's information/communication because he is identified in the Gospel of John as 'Logos,' God's Word sent to us. (John 1:1-5)

7. Finally, just as visible light is a **small part** of the huge EM spectrum (spanning 23 (24?) decades), what we see of God's revelation in Jesus Christ is *"...but a poor reflection of what we will see face to face in heaven."* (1 Corinthians 13:12) Also in 1 Corinthians 2:9 the Apostle Paul quotes from Isaiah 64:4, *"Eye has not seen and ear has not heard, no mind has conceived what God has prepared for those who love him."* We see with our eyes very little of the 'light' around us. What if we insisted on basing our lives only on what we see? Imagine how little of the world we would be able to understand. In the same way, if we insist on living our lives based only on 'sight' or what we can understand, imagine how limited our knowledge will be.

In summary, Christ shines his light (truth) into our hearts and minds and reveals our deepest secrets. In the Old Testament King David invited God to reveal his inner thoughts in Psalm 139:23. *"Search me O God and know my heart, test me and know my anxious thoughts. See if there is any wicked way in me and lead me in the way everlasting."* Now, because we have the Holy Spirit living in us, we can invite him to also search us. If Christ lives in our hearts, we reflect his beauty and we ourselves become the light of the world. (Matthew 5:14)

Fun with Science

✓ **Electromagnetic waves:** Watch two video segments that explain more about the physics of electromagnetic waves, including the scientific theory that couples electricity and magnetism, which is the fundamental principle behind electromagnetic radiation.

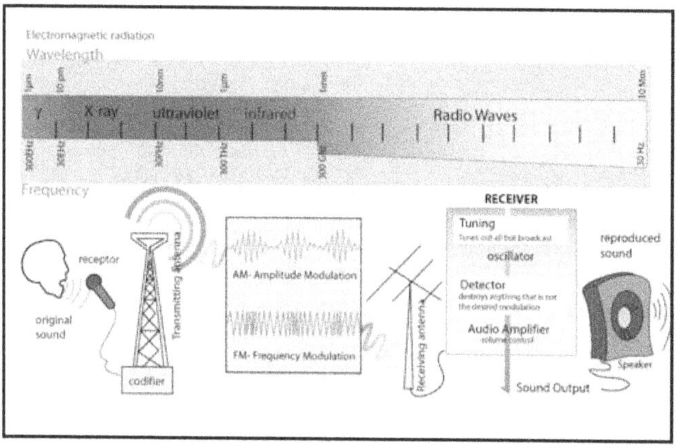

Go to: www.teachersdomain.org (Your parents or teacher can register on this site and use their wonderful educational material over time.) Search for Electromagnetic Spectrum (There is a great video prepared by NASA on the subject as well as several other videos.)

After watching this video, sketch a wave, and explain what a wavelength is. Then show that EM frequency is the speed of light divided by the wavelength.

Look at the EM spectrum shown above. What are the five major categories of the EM spectrum?

✓ **Wavelengths:** hold a prism up to the sun and identify the components that make up the visible spectrum. List the colors in order of their wavelength from red to purple. If you don't have a prism, you can use water and a mirror to divide sunlight into its various wavelengths.

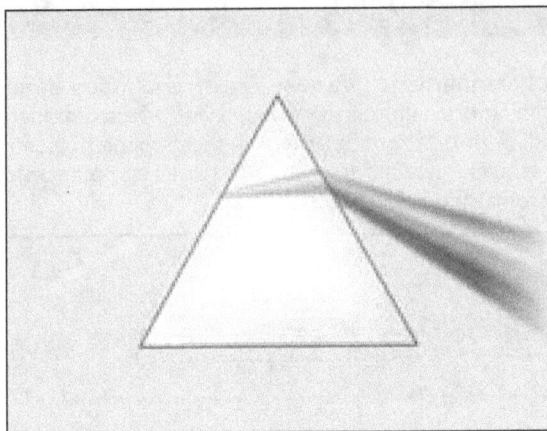

Materials you will need 1. a bowl of fresh water; 2. a small mirror; 3. a piece of white or beige paper; 4. direct sunlight.

Wear sunglasses! Prop up the mirror in the bowl of water so that it is mostly underwater and reflects sunlight. Hold the paper above the mirror so that it captures the reflection. Can you see the colors of the rainbow appear? WARNING: *Do not look directly into the mirror as it could damage your eyes. Never look directly into the sun because the sunlight will burn your eyes and can permanently damage your eyesight.*

As the sunlight passes from air into water and then back into the air, it bends or refracts. Different colors in the sunlight bend at different angles, so the colors separate. When the reflection hits the paper, you see the wavelengths of sunlight separated out—which is a rainbow.

Ultraviolet Light: Get a UV lamp/flashlight or black light (you can order these at the science websites mentioned before). Examine items around your house, shining the black light on them in a dark place. Look at things like white paper, powdered clothes soap, talcum powder, club soda/tonic water, etc. Which items glow under UV light? What causes the glow? How is this glow different from 'glow-in-the-dark' toys that need to be excited by sunlight or bright light bulbs?

Luminescence: This is the property of some materials to absorb energy from light and then reemit it or 'glow' at another wavelength. There are many kinds of luminescence. Luminescence can be caused by UV as well as other radiations, including x-rays, visible light, infrared. Essentially the energy from the UV knocks an electron into a higher energy level (orbits further from nucleus). This electron displacement is balanced by an outer shell electron moving in to fill the gap. The energy given off by this replacement electron is radiated as photons, which appear to us as visible light.

Phosphorescence: This is a chemical reaction of phosphorus materials that takes place when the molecules are excited by UV radiation and then reemit it as visible light. With most fluorescent substances, once the light source is taken away, the electrons settle back into their orbits and there is no further radiation. But in some materials, electrons are so slow in returning to their normal states that the atoms continue to give off light long after the radiative light source has been removed—this is the phenomenon you see with glow-in-the-dark toys.

For more information: see luminescence/phosphorescence on Wikipedia.

There is a general category of rocks called fluorescent rocks. However, it is specific minerals in the rocks that make them glow under UV, including calcite, fluorite, gypsum, agate, and many others.

Science Trivia: Next time you see a double rainbow note the order of the colors. The lower and brighter rainbow goes from violet up to red. The upper or dimmer rainbow goes in the reverse order. Why is this?

Answer: Sun enters raindrops for a primary rainbow near the top of the drops and then reflect off the back of the drop to be seen by people on earth. For the secondary bow however, sun enters the drops of water from below and then reflect off the back two times before emerging or refracting. Since the rays cross over twice inside the drop of water, the colors are reversed when they emerge.

God is Truth

"Jesus answered, "I am the way, the truth and the life. No one comes to the Father except through me."

John 14:6

"What is truth?"

Before being crucified, Christ went through several so-called trials in order to put a veneer of legality on his crucifixion. During his trial before Pontius Pilate, he was asked, *"Are you a king or not?" Jesus answered, "You tell me. Because I am King, I was born and entered the world so that I could witness to the truth. Everyone who cares for truth, who has any feeling for the truth, recognizes my voice." Pilate said, "What is truth?"* (John 18:36-38)

Unfortunately, instead of waiting for Christ's answer, Pilate turned to continue his work of prosecuting Jesus. Too often people don't really seek truth but quickly turn back to their busy lives and just accept what is being said around them. It is very important to really seek out truth because everything in our lives depends on it.

Truth is defined as that which corresponds to reality. If I see a blue ball in the middle of the living room and say, "There is a blue ball in the middle of the living room," that statement is true because others can see the ball and agree with my statement. One of the greatest breakthroughs in human history was the discovery of the Scientific Method (see section 3, chapter 1: "Seeking Treasure; Science Facts: Understanding the Scientific Method"). This process of thinking and testing opened the way for people to discover what is true in nature. Through the Scientific Method the earth's rotation around the sun was discovered, when most people thought the sun rotated around the earth. This process allows other people to examine your thinking and your testing and either agree with your conclusions or disagree, not because they like you or on't like you, but because they find something in your method or thinking that was wrong. The Scientific Method helped to remove hearsay, superstition and mythology from our thinking and has led to the huge advances in science and technology we see today.

There is truth also in the supernatural realm, but it is not as readily testable. Or rather it is not as testable as the rigorous scientific method requires. But nevertheless, it is testable. Jesus said, *"If you stick with this, living out what I tell you, you are my disciples for sure. Then you will experience for yourselves the truth and the truth will set you free."* (John 8:32, *The Message*) Those who listen to and obey Jesus will be able to know spiritual truth (reality) more and more. God is not afraid of being tested, if it is done with a sincerely seeking heart. He invites us to question him. *"Come let us reason together...."* (Isaiah 1:18) The Apostle John, when writing to the church, says, *"We proclaim to you what we have seen and heard"* (1 John 1:3) He is saying that there is evidence for what he is saying and preaching, tangible evidence. Finally, Jesus said, *"I am the truth"* (John 14:6) If we want to know truth in the supernatural realm, we must come to know Jesus—what he taught, who he was and what he asks us to do and be.

Are the horizontal lines straight or at an angle? Can we always believe what we see?

Science Facts: Understanding the Philosophical Issues in Science

All truth is God's truth. In the physical world, we find truths in many human endeavors: physical, social, ethical, etc. These truth claims are arrived at after much testing and evaluating before finally applying them to real life situations. In science, truth claims are considered tentative until they are tested carefully by many scientists, independently verified over time, and eventually accepted as part of physical reality.

Many human activities, however, are not subject to empirical testing as required by the strict rules of the scientific method. Nevertheless, they remain as truths by which we live: for example, knowing that your family loves you, caring about other people, music, art, etc.

There has been a move away from truth in Western culture in recent years. People believe that there is no such thing as something being really true, or absolutely true. Truth varies according to the situation or is based on the experience of those who proclaim it. Truth is seen as a means to power. However, there is a fundamental contradiction in this way of thinking. When someone claims that all truth is relative, they are making an absolute statement. This statement is self-contradictory.

Science is a human activity that has its own boundaries because it deals with empirical data that is repeatable, empirically testable, and allows the scientist to make predictions. When scientists begin to claim that truth can only be known through the scientific method, this is a statement of faith and is called scientism. Scientism is the belief that science can discover all truth, even truth that cannot be tested. Those who believe in scientism think that every question can ultimately be answered by science and therefore, we have no need for god or anything supernatural. Here are five important points that every person should keep in mind, when doing good science (Reference 6):

1. Science continually raises philosophical questions that go beyond the competence or purview of science.

2. Evidence of random chemical processes is not necessarily evidence for philosophical accidentalism.

3. In science, an unanswered question is far more important than an unquestioned answer.

4. In science, tentative conclusions should be stated in tentative form.

5. The confidence expressed in any scientific conclusion should be directly proportional to the quantity and quality of evidence for that conclusion.

These are sober reminders that the scientific method has its own limitations and boundaries, when searching for truth in nature. Beyond those boundaries are legitimate human activities that teach us of truths that are historical, philosophical, religious, etc. The most unusual claim about truth is the statement made by Christ in answer to Thomas' question (given in the verse at the beginning of this chapter), when he identified himself as Ultimate Truth. In saying this Jesus Christ identified himself as part of the godhead.

There have been and are today many outstanding scientists who have been both innovators in their field of science and deeply committed Christian believers. Below is a partial list that includes the field of science to which each has made significant breakthroughs.

Copernicus	(1473-1543)	Heliocentric
Tycho Brahe & Kepler	(1571-1630)	Elliptic Orbits
Galileo Galilei	(1564-1642)	Evidence: Jupiter & It's Orbits
Newton	(1642-1727)	Classical Physics
Faraday	(1791-1867)	Electricity
Maxwell	(1831-1879)	Electromagnetic Theory
Boyle	(1627-1691)	Chemistry as Science
Lord Kelvin	(1824-1907)	Thermodynamics
Planck	(1858-1947)	Quantum Mechanics
Smalley	(1943-2005)	Nanotechnology
Townes, Charles	(1915-)	Invented Mazers and Lasers
Phillips, William	(1948-)	Laser Cooling & Trapping of Atoms
Collins, Francis	(1950-)	Leader of the Human Genome Project

* Actually, when we use the Scientific Method to understand and explain how nature functions, the most we can do is to model natural phenomena rather than fully grasp reality itself. As finite human beings, our understanding is limited by the complexity and vastness of all that one can know.

Fun with Science:

To further investigate and/or understand some of the issues being raised today in the field of science and faith, you can visit the following websites:

- www.veritas.org

   This is the website of Veritas, a Christian ministry that focuses on graduate students. They bring some of the top Christian intellectuals to speak on relevant topics, many of which are related to science and faith. Many of these lectures are available on the website in video format.

- www.aaas.org

   This is the premier website for scientists around the world. The AAAS (American Association for the Advancement of Science) publishes the highly regarded magazine, Science. AAAS recently initiated a dialogue devoted to issues related to science and faith. The AAAS has a history of strongly supporting the secular, naturalist position. Their recent action indicates that the importance of religion among scientists. In 2010 a young woman was appointed to lead this effort called the Dialogue on Science, Ethics and Religion. Her name is Dr. Jennifer Wiseman and she is an outspoken Christian as well as an astrophysicist with a Ph.D. from Harvard.

Dr Francis Collins, who was appointed as Director of the National Institute of Health (NIH) by President Obama in 2009, has also been very open about his Christian faith and some of his testimony can be found on YouTube.

Part II

Who Am I?

I am Unique; I Belong

"You created my inmost being;
you knit me together in my mother's womb."

Psalm 139:13

Belonging to a group is very important for humans. God has made us for relationship. Our most important relationship is with Him, but he has also given us the joy of other human relationships. We have relationships with our family, with our mother and father, our grandparents and our brothers and sisters. Each of us belongs to a community, whether it is our town, our neighborhood, our church, or our school or our sports team. These relationships bring us happiness and help us understand who we are.

However, there are some people who have been rejected in all their relationships, sometimes because of bad choices they have made. People on drugs or alcohol usually have few people who care for them. People in prison are very restricted in their relationships. Sometimes when you are chronically sick you don't have many friends. Some people are rejected because of something they cannot control, like the color of their skin, or the place they are from, or certain disabilities.

In Jesus' day there were people who were rejected by their communities. At that time, Jews considered it very important to keep the law. Those who did not keep the law were considered unclean and were rejected. However, the religious leaders who kept the law, called Pharisees, were very proud of their goodness and looked down on people who did not obey the laws, like they did. They would not even touch these 'bad' people for fear of becoming unclean. One day Jesus was invited to have dinner with one of these Pharisees named Simon. It was the custom at that time to offer water to wash the feet of guests when they came to your house, because everyone walked and the roads were dusty. But Simon did not think Jesus was very important and did not offer him any water for washing before they sat down to eat.

"Just then a woman of the village, the town harlot (a very bad lady), having learned that Jesus was a guest in the home of the Pharisee, came with a bottle of very expensive perfume and stood at his feet, weeping, raining tears on his feet. Letting down her hair, she dried his feet, kissed them, and anointed them with perfume.

When the Pharisee who had invited him saw this, he said to himself, "If this man was the prophet I thought he was, he would have known what kind of woman this is who is falling all over him."

Jesus said to him, "Simon, I have something to tell you."

"Oh? Tell me."

"Two men were in debt to a banker. One owed five hundred silver pieces, the other fifty. Neither of them could pay up, and so the banker canceled both debts. Which of the two would be more grateful?"

Simon answered, "I suppose the one who was forgiven the most."

"That's right," said Jesus. Then turning to the woman, but speaking to Simon, he said, "Do you see this woman? I came to your home; you provided no water for my feet, but she rained tears on my

feet and dried them with her hair. You gave me no greeting, but from the time I arrived she hasn't quit kissing my feet. You provided nothing for freshening up, but she has soothed my feet with perfume. Impressive, isn't it? She was forgiven many, many sins, and so she is very, very grateful. If the forgiveness is minimal, the gratitude is minimal."

Then he spoke to her: "I forgive your sins.... Your faith has saved you. Go in peace." Luke 7:36-50 (The Message)

Even though this woman was rejected by the people around her, Jesus welcomed her and forgave her sins. God has made each of us unique, with a unique 'secret code', a unique environment in which to grow, a unique purpose in life and a unique way to relate to Him. We really are "fearfully and wonderfully made." (Psalm 139:14) God loves each unique person and has provided a way for us to relate to Him and to belong to His Family—the Family of God.

Science Facts: Understanding DNA

Nature's most amazing secret code goes by the name DNA. It is the genetic code within the cells of every living organism. The genetic code is made up of DNA, which stands for Deoxyribonucleic acid and is the blueprint for the construction of cells. As human beings we each are made up of trillions (a thousand billion) of cells and our DNA has a special code for the construction of each type of cell that makes up our body. Each cell controls hundreds of millions of biochemical and biomechanical events per cell cycle, some processing as fast as 1000 nucleotides (the GCAT building blocks) per second, with very few mistakes. There are about 2 meters (6 feet) of DNA in **each** of our cells. The DNA in each cell contains about 750 megabytes of data, equivalent to hundreds of volumes of instructions. Our DNA is packaged up into 'chromosomes', two tiny, closely-linked strands in each cell nucleus. Every person's DNA is about 99% the same. It is the 1% difference that makes each of us so unique.

The DNA is in the shape of a twisted ladder, made up of rungs on the ladder, each consisting of 40 molecules using only four "letters" GCAT. These are called base pairs—C only pairs up with G, and T only pairs up with A. There are about 3 billion base pairs in each DNA. These four molecules are put together in a code that can be used to create...YOU.

The Code of Life

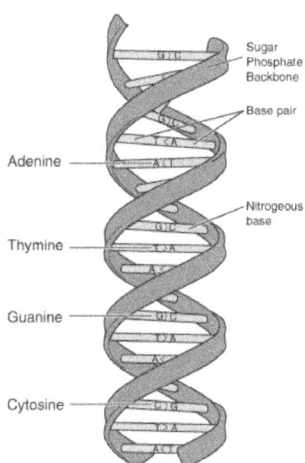

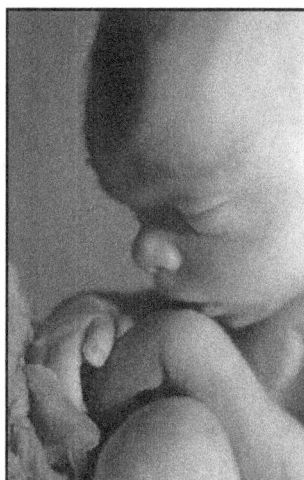

Baby in the Womb at 24 Weeks

Insights from God's Two Books

Who am I? Did you know that this is a very important question? As you grow older it is important that you are able to answer this question with understanding; otherwise someone or something will try to tell you who you are. If you don't know who you are based on God's truth, you will believe what people tell you even when it is a lie. So in this chapter we want to consider the question of who you are from the perspective of the one who created you—your Heavenly Father.

In Genesis 2, the Bible gives us the story of man's creation. God created Adam from the dust of the ground and then breathed into him the breath of life. This indicates that we humans consist of a body (dust) which is from the earth and in many ways resembles the bodies of the other animals. We also have a spirit, the breath of God, and have capacities far beyond that of animals.

According to Darwin's Theory of Evolution, the chimpanzees are 'our nearest relatives.' The DNA of the chimpanzee is very close to that of human beings (96%). Those who do not believe in the creation story tell us that we share a common ancestor with the chimpanzee and site as proof the similarity of our DNA. God made both the chimp and the human being from the dust of the earth and therefore, even the Bible agrees that physically we are very close to the animal world, including chimpanzees. And yet there is a huge difference between what a chimp can do and what man does, because we bear the image of God. Here is a partial list of what makes man unique from the whole animal world.

- only man uses language to communicate ideas

- only man makes advanced tools

- only man has set up laws

- only man has developed cultural traditions

- only man engages in ritual

- only man has a moral conscience

  (based on a list compiled by Sir Mortimer Adler in *Ten Philosophical Mistakes*, Reference 7)

So God has given humans a unique place in the cosmos. He has also made you unique. The DNA is so complicated that no one person will ever have the same DNA as another, even with billions of people. There is no one else in the world like you, with your special set of interests, talents, experiences, But even more amazing, you have a unique genetic code that is different from every other person who ever lived.

Fun with Science

✓ *Create a paper model of DNA.* DNA looks like a twisted ladder, made up of the four "letters," G, C, A, and T. As stated above, these are called base pairs, with C pairing up with G and T pairing up with A.

Fun model creation instructions can be found at:

- www.csiro.au/resources/dna-model-template.html

- www.starsandseas.com/SAS%20Cells/DNA%20Replication/dnarepli_model.htm

✓ *Conduct a DNA extraction experiment using household chemicals, strawberries, bananas or other foods.*

Materials needed:

- zip lock bags
- strawberries, bananas (can also try onions, broccoli, chicken liver, kiwis, and other common foods)
- gauze (large gauze squares)
- funnels and test tubes
- ice cold ethanol or isopropyl rubbing alcohol
- cocktail sticks
- shampoo or dishwashing detergent
- salt
- measuring cups, measuring spoons or graduated cylinders
- small glass jars or clear cups to store results

Make DNA extraction buffer:

To make 500 ml of extraction buffer, mix 50 ml shampoo or 25 ml dishwashing detergent with
7.5 g (1 teaspoon) kitchen salt and 450 ml water.

To extract DNA:

1. Wash strawberries and remove leaves. Peel and chop up bananas.

2. Crush strawberries or bananas in a plastic Ziploc bag with your hands. If you want to set a control for your experiment, make two bags for each extraction.

3. Add two teaspoonfuls of extraction solution (mentioned above) to the extraction bag, but **not** to the control bag. Seal the bag and squeeze it for a minute or two to get it well mixed in the bag.

Crushing up the bananas and strawberries breaks open the cells of the fruits. The **enzymes** *in the soap (from the detergent or the shampoo) break down the lipid molecules in the cell and nucleus membranes, releasing the contents of the cell, including DNA into the solution. These are the same enzymes that break down the grease when you wash the dishes. The positives charges provided by the* **salt** *neutralize the negatively charged DNA and allow it to clump together.*

4. Cut the gauze and place it into a funnel and put funnel into test tube. Prepare one for each extraction and control.

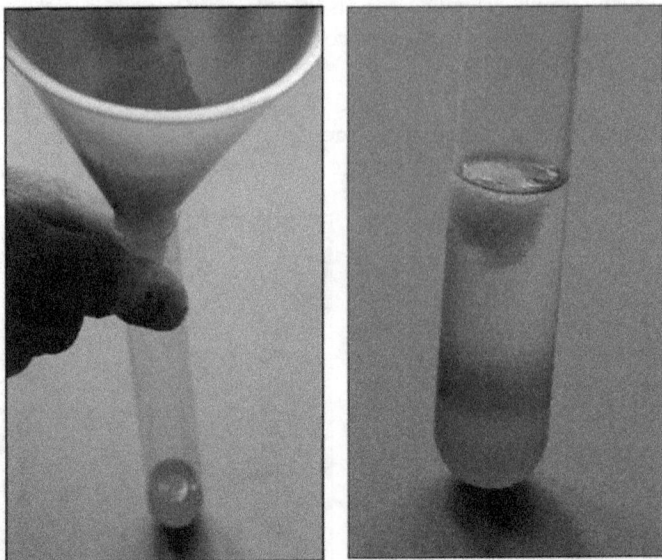

5. Pour the smashed fruit mixture on into the gauze and filter the mixture through the funnel into the test tube. You can mash it down with a spoon, but be careful not to let any large chunks into the test tube.

The gauze is filtering out the cell debris and large pieces, allowing only the DNA to pass through to the test tube. Strawberry solutions should be bright red.

6. Remove the funnel and carefully pour ice cold ethanol into the extraction test tube until it is about half full. Do the same with the control. The ethanol should form a layer on top of the filtrate.

7. Do not shake or stir the test tubes, just look carefully to watch what happens. You should see a cluster of rope-like substances floating in the alcohol layer in the extraction test tube—these are millions of DNA molecules clustered together. Compare these results with the control test tube. The control helps you decide if what you are seeing is really DNA or just strawberry goo.

DNA does not dissolve in alcohol (unlike the cell debris), so it precipitates out of solution. DNA is less dense than water so it floats into the alcohol layer.

8. If you would like to preserve your DNA for a while, scoop it out with a cocktail stick and put it in a small clear container with a little bit of alcohol. In a tightly sealed container, it can be stable for a long time.

Note that strawberries are especially well suited for this experiment because they are octoploid—they have eight copies of each chromosome—and thus lots of DNA to extract! Human body cells are diploid, which means they only have two copies of each chromosome.

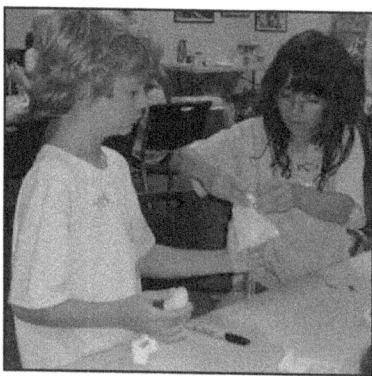

I am Bought with a Price

"The Son of Man did not come to be served, but to serve,
and to give his life as a ransom for many."
Matthew 20:28

From earliest human history, blood has symbolized life. Many cultures have practiced blood sacrifice, usually using the blood of animals but sometimes also the blood of humans, as in the case of the Aztec Indians of Central America. The Bible has consistently used the symbol of blood to represent life and there are many verses in the Old Testament that forbid the drinking of blood (Leviticus 3:17; 7:26; 17:11, 14 and others), because it would be like drinking the life of another creature.

Blood in the Bible also symbolizes cleansing. It has been used in sacrifices to make a person acceptable before God, or clean. This seems strange since blood stains clothes and is messy. But blood was used to cleanse or heal lepers (Lev. 14:1-7) and to make the Israelites acceptable before God. When the Israelites worshipped God, it always involved killing bulls or sheep or goats and sprinkling their blood on the altar in the Temple. The priests would offer the blood or life of these animals to God instead of killing the actual person who had sinned. In this way the blood of animals was a substitute for human blood, or death.

When the children of Israel were preparing to escape from Egypt, God told them to kill a lamb and put the blood on their doorposts. The Angel of Death would be coming through the country and would kill the first-born child in each house unless he saw the blood on the doorpost. Only the blood of an animal was able to save the Israelites from God's curse of death. The name for the Jewish festival 'Passover' comes from this event. The angel of death would 'pass over' the house that had blood on its doorposts.

Finally, when Jesus came to earth to live among men and women, he knew that he would be killed as a sacrifice for the sin of the people. *"The Son of Man did not come to be served, but to serve, and to give his life as a ransom for many."* (Matt. 20:28) Just like the high priest went into the Holy Place in the Jewish Temple to offer up animal blood on the sacred altar for the sins of the people, so Jesus went into the heavenly Temple to offer up blood. However, he did not offer up the blood of animals. He offered up his own blood. *"When the real thing takes place, these animal sacrifices (from Jewish tradition) aren't needed any more, having served their purpose. For Christ didn't enter the earthly version of the Holy Place; he entered the Place Itself, and offered himself to God as the sacrifice for our sins...He sacrificed himself once and for all, summing up all the other sacrifices in this sacrifice of himself, the final solution of sin."* Hebrews 9: 24-26 (The Message)

That is why Christians celebrate the sacrament of Communion, or the Lord's Supper. Jesus Christ commanded his disciples to remember his death often, by taking bread and wine, which symbolize his body and blood. At the Last Supper, before his death, Jesus said, *"This is the new covenant in my blood, which is poured out for you."* Luke 22:20

Science Facts: Understanding the Functions of Blood

The two primary functions of blood are to supply the body's cells with needed nutrients and oxygen and to carry waste products away from those same cells. In its waste removal capacity, blood is the most wonderful cleansing agent in nature. Blood is both the body's supplier and janitor. In order for it to function in this capacity, blood must be in touch with every cell in the body. It travels to every cell through arteries, then arterioles, then tiny capillaries which altogether are over 50,000 miles long. In only one day, a blood cell travels 12,000 miles! After it deposits the supplies (nutrients and oxygen) and picks up the waste (carbon dioxide (CO_2) and metabolites), it returns to the central pumping station (the heart) via the veins. The right side of the heart then pumps this blood to the lungs so that it can dump the carbon dioxide and pick up more oxygen. After this cycle, blood returns to the heart where the left side pumps the oxygenated blood to the body. This process of moving blood through the body is called circulation (pulmonary and systemic).

Imagine a giant pipeline over 50,000 miles long which snakes through every jungle village in South America, under the Atlantic Ocean, throughout Africa and up through the cities of Europe, across Russia and China, under the Pacific Ocean and finally to North America. This pipeline carries everything humans need: food, electronics, clothing, furniture, and everything one could find in a mall. Anyone of the six billion people on earth can reach in and take what they need. Immediately, that item will be replaced in the pipeline. This will give you an idea of how amazing the circulatory system is.

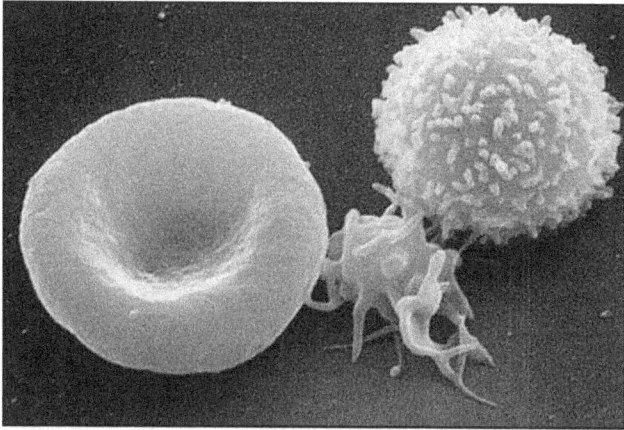

Left to right: erythrocyte (red blood cell), platelet, leukocyte (white blood cell) (Wikimedia Commons)

Blood is the liquid that flows through this pipeline. It consists of blood cells (red blood cells and white blood cells), and platelets suspended in a liquid called plasma. The red blood cells do not have a nucleus, but instead have a molecule called hemoglobin, a protein that binds with the oxygen molecule making it much more soluble in blood. Carbon dioxide in contrast is transported in the plasma as a bicarbonate ion. Red blood cells have a tough life, constantly loading and unloading their cargo. After about 250,000 trips through the circulatory system, they are worn out. At this stage they return to the bone marrow where they were first manufactured. Here they are taken apart and recycled to produce new red blood cells. Four million red cells per second retire to this junkyard and at the same time, four million new cells are loaded into the blood stream, ready to go to work again.

A tiny dot of blood contains over five million red blood cells, 300,000 platelets and 7,000 white blood cells. The red cells are the work horses of the blood, supplying the trillions of cells that make up the adult human body, with everything they need. The white cells are the warriors, ready to attack anything deemed an enemy. The platelets are the nurses, with a ready first-aid box. They are critical to the process of clotting. Without them, any injury could result in death since the blood would never stop flowing. So together these cells detect leaks and enemies, rush to the rescue, and clean up after the disaster.

The kidney is the organ that filters out poisons from the blood. With each heartbeat, about one gallon of blood flows through the kidney. The kidney extracts the sugars, salts and water from the red blood cells (because they are too big to fit through the tubules) and runs this liquid through its 2,000,000 tiny tubules. After the filtering process, the kidney reinserts about 99% of the volume back into the blood stream. The 1 % remaining is sent to the bladder to be expelled from the body. All of this happens with each heartbeat.

Finally, the heart! This amazing pump faithfully moves blood through the body for an average of 2,500,000 cycles (about 35 million beats a year during a 75-year life expectancy). It usually requires no maintenance and weighs about 300 grams. It pumps about 2,000 gallons per day, and during a normal life expectancy it pumps 1 million barrels of blood, enough to fill three super tankers! No machine developed by humans has been able to match its capacity.

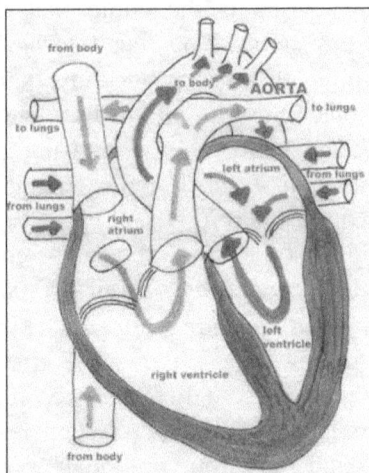

Insights from God's Two Books

In our modern society where most of us live in cities, we feel a bit squeamish about blood. We associate it with bad things like wounds, murder and sickness. But even in our culture, blood has both a positive and negative aspect. "Give the Gift of Life: Donate Blood" says a poster seeking volunteers for blood donations. But when there are graphic pictures on TV depicting a crime scene or natural disaster, we are told to turn away. In this case, blood means death.

In the Jewish culture blood was everywhere, from the daily routine of feeding a household using local animals to the annual religious festivals where thousands of animals were killed for temple sacrifices. God taught his people using the symbol of blood even before science discovered the chemical processes that take place in the circulatory system. The physical properties of blood serve as wonderful examples of the spiritual process that takes place when we are forgiven, cleansed and given power through our trust in Christ.

Blood (the red blood cells or erythrocytes) does two jobs: provide oxygen and nutrients to the cells and removes waste products and toxins. Jesus Christ asked his disciples to symbolically drink his blood during the Last Supper. *"He took the cup, gave thanks, and offered it to them, saying, Drink from it, all of you. This is my blood of the covenant, which is poured out for many for the forgiveness of sins."* (Matthew 26:27) This was a shock to his disciples, since Jews were strictly forbidden to drink blood, because life was in the blood. By this graphic symbol, Jesus was teaching that when we trust in him and submit to him, we actually take his "life" (or blood) into ourselves. Forgiveness can be compared to the process of removing the poison or toxin from our life. Things like pride, selfishness, greed, grumbling, and gossip are removed by the presence of Christ in our lives. Repentance can be compared to the way each cell interacts with the blood to allow the toxins to be removed. In the same way, we need to allow and even invite the work of the Holy Spirit to take sin away. We need to be willing. Finally, the Holy Spirit brings life-giving nutrients to our souls, like peace, joy, love and hope. These are like oxygen to our cells; they give us energy and life.

Christians today usually take the 'cross' as their symbol. The 'cross' is associated with the death of Christ which paid the price for our acceptance by the Heavenly Father. But the early church chose another symbol—the fish! The first Christians were persecuted and knew too much about death. They wanted to celebrate life. The most common symbol found in the catacombs near Rome, where Christians hid and often died, was the fish. The fish symbol is called: Ichthys (ΙΧΘΥΣ), which means 'fish' in Greek. Each of the letters stands for the name of Jesus Christ. The fish symbol also was used to help Christians identify each other, using a secret code. The first person would draw:

If the second person was a believer, he would complete the picture:

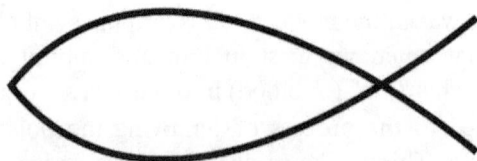

In these two symbols, the 'cross' and the 'fish' we are reminded of the meaning of 'blood.' Blood can symbolize both 'death' and 'life.' God has given us an amazing living example of a spiritual reality.

I = Iota = Iesous = Jesus
X = chi = Christos = Christ
Θ= Theta = Theou = God's
Υ = Upsilon = Yios = Son
Σ = Sigma = Soter = Savior

Fun with Science

What happens when your muscles don't get blood?

To really understand the cleansing power of blood, find a blood pressure cuff. Wrap it around your upper arm and inflate until there is no blood flowing to your lower arm. At first, you will feel tightness around the cuff. Now try doing a simple task like flexing your fingers and making a fist about ten times, or cut paper with scissors. Quickly you will start to feel weakness. Suddenly a hot flash of pain will strike. Your muscles will cramp. If you continue, you will likely cry out in agony. Finally, you cannot continue no matter how hard you try. Then release the tight cuff. Blood will rush into your aching arm and your muscles will begin to relax and the pain will subside. You have just experienced the cleansing power of blood, as it rushed in to remove the toxins and supply your cells with oxygen.

Simple chemistry experiment to illustrate the cleansing power of Christ's blood.

Supplies:
- Cornstarch
- Vinegar
- Tincture of iodine
- Sodium carbonate (Na_2CO_3), which can be found in "pH plus" for increasing pool/spa pH, or washing soda
- Sodium thiosulphate ($Na_2S_2O_3$), found in aquarium dechlorinators/water conditioners, and in photographer's fixing "hypo" solution.
- pH indicator solution (red solution found with pool supplies)
- 1 L beakers (2)

Mix up two solutions:

- Cornstarch and vinegar solution
    1. 2.7g (one teaspoon) of cornstarch to 500 ml (1 pint) of <u>cold</u> water.
    2. Mix one part vinegar to four parts cornstarch solution (example: approximately 10 ml vinegar to 40 ml starch solution). Final solution should be white.

- Indicator solution*
  1. Add the pH indicator solution to water (1/2 to 1 cup) and if the water is neutral, it should turn red. If needed, you could try to adjust the pH by using a tiny speck of "pH plus" for spas or washing soda.
  2. Add a few squirts of aquarium water conditioner (Thiosulphate solution) to the red water.
  3. For the demonstration, add a few drops of iodine to the cornstarch/vinegar solution. It will turn black. Add the red pH indicator to water in separate beaker, then the aquarium water conditioner. When the red solution is added to the black solution, the final solution should return to its original 'whiteish' color.

Note: this experiment may need some adjustments depending on your water and the chemicals you use.

Spiritual Illustration:

The cornstarch-vinegar solution represents the heart of man at Creation before sin entered the world-white. The bottle (of iodine) represents sin. Iodine taken internally is deadly poison, just as sin is to our souls. When Adam and Eve listened to the serpent and disobeyed God, sin entered their hearts. Drop a few drops of iodine into the cornstarch-vinegar solution and gently stir—the liquid should turn a blue-black color (iodine complexes with amylase molecules in starch). Because of sin, man lost his holiness and his spiritual life with God and was doomed to eternal death.

But God loved us so much that he planned a way for man to be saved. God sent Jesus to earth. Jesus died on the cross and shed his blood for us so that we might have eternal life. The Bible tells us that if we believe in Jesus and ask Him into our hearts and if we confess our sins and ask Jesus to forgive us, He will make our hearts white and pure again. Pour the red liquid into the black liquid—the final liquid should be whiteish in color. (*The thiosulfate discharges the blue-black color of the iodine, and acidic vinegar discharges the red color of the pH indicator).* The blood of Jesus cleanses us from all sin.

I Can Be Transformed

"We who…reflect the Lord's glory are being transformed into his likeness."
2 Corinthians 3:1

Transformation is a big word that means to change form. You can buy toys called "Transformers" that change form and nature. For example, one can change from a car into a robot. That is a change in both form or shape and in nature or purpose. A robot has a very different shape and purpose from a car. God's Word has a lot to say about transformation. When we begin our journey trusting Christ, we also begin a journey of transformation. The Apostle Paul also wrote, *"If anyone is in Christ, he is a new creation."* (2 Corinthians 5:17)

One of the most amazing examples of transformation in the Bible is the story of the Apostle Paul, told in Acts 9:1-31. His original name was Saul, and he was a powerful Jewish religious leader. He tried very hard to keep all the commandments and wanted to keep the Jewish religion pure. That is why he hated the early believers in Jesus. They were saying that God loves the world through Jesus and that more than keeping the commandments, God wanted people to love and trust him and to believe in his son, Jesus. This got Saul very angry and he traveled around the country persecuting believers, putting them into prison and even killing them.

But an amazing transformation happened to him. Jesus met Saul as he was traveling to Damascus to kill more believers, and told him that when he persecuted believers, he was persecuting Jesus. Suddenly Saul's eyes were opened and he realized that Jesus really was the Son of God. When he believed, Jesus changed his name from Saul to Paul and gave him the very important ministry of taking the message of God's love through Jesus to the world. Paul spent the rest of his life traveling and sharing this message. He had many hardships and in the end, he was imprisoned and killed. But the Apostle Paul never regretted his transformation from one who tried to stop others from believing in Jesus, to one who tried to help others believe in Jesus. Paul said in Philippians 3:8, *"I consider everything a loss compared to the surpassing greatness of knowing Christ Jesus my Lord."*

Science Facts: Understanding the Photovoltaic (PV) Process

All life on earth is dependent on the sun. The sun sends out tremendous amounts of energy, providing us with light and heat, helping plants grow, and warming the earth. Did you know that we can take the sun's energy (called solar energy) and turn it into energy that we can use (electricity)? This is the purpose of a solar panel. A solar panel is a large flat rectangle, typically somewhere between the size of a radiator and the size of a door, made up of many individual solar energy collectors called solar cells.

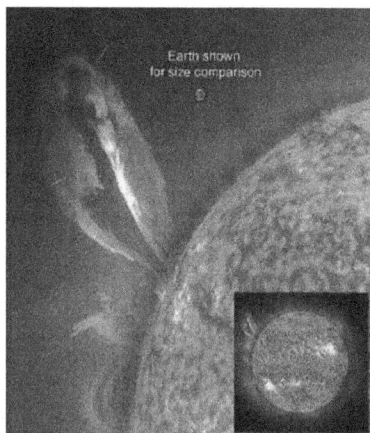

Earth shown for size comparison

Just like cells in a battery, the cells in a solar panel are designed to generate electricity; but whereas a battery's cells make electricity from chemicals, a solar panel's cells generate power by capturing sunlight instead. They are sometimes called photovoltaic cells because they use sunlight ("photo" comes from the Greek word for light) to make electricity (the word voltaic is a reference to electricity pioneer Alessandro Volta).

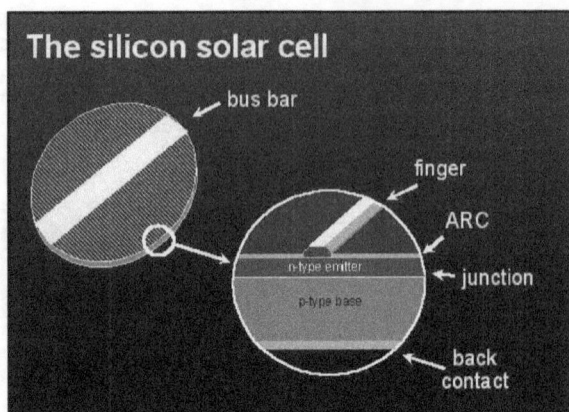

The silicon solar cell

bus bar

finger

ARC

n-type emitter

p-type base

junction

back contact

We see sand everywhere, especially when we go to the beach. Sand is made up of the chemical element silicon. Solar cells are also made from silicon. When sunlight shines on a solar cell, the energy it carries knocks electrons out of the silicon atom and creates an electron-hole pair in an electric field. The current created will thus flow around a circuit and power anything that runs on electricity. Sand that cannot generate electricity is transformed into silicon wafers, which are capable of generating electricity. There are several steps needed to bring about that transformation.

Amonix 35kW concentrator PV module

From Sand to Solar Cell

The mono-crystalline Si cell and the poly crystalline Si cell have a crystalline structure that is highly purified. The cell has been prepared from simple sand or quartzite (silicon dioxide, SiO2) and can respond to light, converting light (the photons that make up light) into electricity.

The sand must be purified at 1410° C (2000° F) by melting it and removing all the impurities. After purification (about 99.9999% pure silicon), two elements referred to as 'donor' and 'acceptor' elements are added to the silicon. They are boron and phosphorus. These additives enhance the generation of current in the circuit.

The expert uses a process that is energy intensive and therefore, very expensive. Sand and quartzite are relatively inexpensive, but the manufactured silicon wafer is not. As of 2009, a typical watt of power from a PV (photovoltaic) Si cell costs $3.

There are many types of solar cells. The most common these days is the single crystal or poly-silicon cell. These cells respond to sunlight or desk lamps where the light is towards the red color (spectrum). If you use a fluorescent lamp instead, the silicon solar cell will not respond, because fluorescent light is more toward the blue color of the spectrum.

Insights from God's Two Books

The Bible says that we *"are dust and to dust we shall return"* (Genesis 3:19). Our bodies are made up of minerals and chemicals that are common on the earth. But God has also given us a soul (*nephesh* in Hebrew = breath) so that we can have a relationship with God, who is spirit. God transforms our soul, just like we can transform sand, and makes us more and more like him. Here are some lessons we can learn about transformation from the solar cell.

1. Purification: Just as the sand (silicon) must be purified at 1410°C (2000°F), melting it and removing all the impurities, so our innermost being must be purified from sin. *"I will sprinkle clean water on you, and you will be clean; I will cleanse you from all your impurities"* (Ezekiel 36:25).

2. Receptors Added: After purification, two elements are added to the silicon so that it can use the photons from the sun's light to produce electricity. When we choose to follow Christ, God gives us his Spirit which works in our hearts and minds to transform us from the inside out, helping us understand God's Word and our own hearts. *"I will remove from you your heart of stone and give you a heart of flesh."* (Ezekiel 36:26).

TOURYAN

3. Done by an Expert: The process cannot be done without an expert who is trained in making solar cells. We also cannot transform ourselves. Only the Heavenly Father who made us knows how to change our hearts.

4. Costly: This process of 'sand to solar cell' is a costly process. It does not cost the sand anything but the expert who is transforming the sand has to pay quite a high price for every watt of power. God paid a high price for our transformation. He gave *"his only son so that whoever believes will have eternal life."* *"But God demonstrates his own love for us in this: While we were still sinners, Christ died for us"* (Romans 5:8).

Illustration of how solar energy can make music

One way solar energy can be used is to generate music in a solar music box. You need a 1W photovoltaic cell on which are etched a couple of conductors. The conductors are then connected to an electric motor that runs a musical cylinder. When placed in the sun the conductors send solar-generated electricity to the motor, which turns, turning the musical apparatus, making music.

The solar music box is a great illustration of how the power of the Son of God (Jesus) can transform us (dust of the earth) into people with a new song.

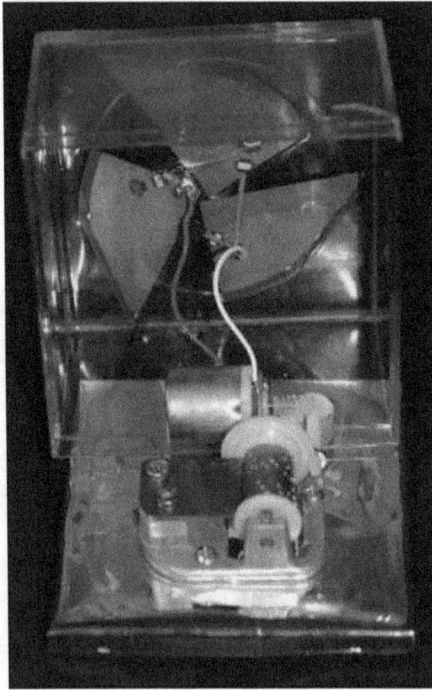

Applications from a Solar Music Box:

1. If you turn the music box such that the light is striking the solar cell at a shallow angle instead of head-on, the song begins to die. To produce the strongest song, the cell should face the in-coming light head-on (perpendicular). This is an illustration of how we must

stay in the light in order for our 'song' to be strong. When we begin to turn away from the light (God), our song (joy and peace) begins to fade.

2. What does it mean to "walk in the light"? [John 8:12; Ephesians 5:8; 1 John 2:9]

3. If you slip a piece of paper or an opaque object between the light source and the solar cell, the song will die. The light is not able to penetrate the cell. In the same way, if we allow something to come between ourselves and God, our joy and peace will begin to die.

4. What would be something that could come between you and Christ, the Light? [Isaiah 59:1, 2; 1 John 1:5-9]

5. Finally, if we place the solar cell in fluorescent light, it will not respond. Fluorescent light is closer to blue light. Silicon does not respond to blue light, but only to red light. In other words, the transformed sand is made to respond to the 'true' light only. This illustrates how God has made us to respond to his love and grace, but if we instead start following another 'light', again our song dies. Other lights can represent things of this world that we begin to want more than God, or spiritual teachings and guides that are not true followers of Christ.

6. What are some other 'lights' that people follow? [1 John 2:15-17; Isaiah 50:11; John 10:5].

Fun with Science

Learning about **solar cells** and using energy from the sun to power a motor.

You can learn much more about solar energy and photovoltaic panels by visiting the U.S. government website at www.nrel.gov. There is a section especially for kids! It directs you to a company that sells solar powered vehicles (www.solarwind.com). There are also other sites that sell kits and/or individual parts to produce your own PV-run motor. *Warning: most of the cheaper kits are very fragile and the PV panels are not very strong so the motor will not run unless it is in direct, strong sunlight. Check out customer reviews before purchasing.*

- www.sundancesolar.com

- www.electronickits.com

- (The Solar Speeder Solaroller is a solid vehicle)

- www.stevespanglerscience.com

- www.solarwind.com

Other educational sites:

- www.californiasolarcenter.org

- www.rahus.org

- www.nrel.gov

If you live in Colorado, the National Renewable Energy Laboratory (in Golden, west of Denver) has a Visitor's Center where one can see demonstration models of many of the newer discoveries in renewable energy.

I am Created to Trust God

*"With all your heart you must trust the LORD…Always let him lead
you, and he will clear the road for you to follow.*

Proverbs 3:5—6 (The Message)

The amazing story of David's battle with the giant Goliath
is part of our spiritual legacy. David was a young man, the
youngest of eight sons, whose job was to guard his family's
sheep. His older brothers along with many other soldiers from
the Israeli army were facing a formidable enemy, the Philistines.
But the most frightening thing about the Philistines was the
giant they had as part of their troops. This giant, Goliath,
challenged the Israeli army to a fight, one-on-one, if they would
select one man to come forth and fight him. Whoever won
would have the right to take the opposite group as slaves. For
forty days Goliath taunted the Israeli troops and they were
terrified. No man volunteered to fight Goliath.

But one day David arrived at the stand-off and saw what
was happening. His father had sent him to the battle to bring
food to his brothers and to find out how they were doing. David
was shocked to see the Israeli troops so afraid of this giant. He
knew that if you trusted in God Jehovah, you did not need to
fear because God would fight for you. David volunteered to go
out and fight the giant. Everyone was afraid for him and told
him he was just a boy and did not know how to fight such a
battle. They even tried to give him some armor which was too
big for him and made it impossible for him to move. But David
remembered that God had helped him when he fought off lions
and bears while guarding the sheep, so he was not afraid.

David got his sling shot and while he walked out to fight the giant, he stopped at a small brook and picked up five smooth, round stones and put them into his shepherd's pouch. He then picked out one and put it in his sling. Goliath was laughing at the size of the 'fighting man' the Israelis had sent out and ranted and raved about how he would make mincemeat of him and feed him to the birds. But David said, *"You come at me with sword and spear and battle-ax. I come at you in the name of God Almighty, the God of Israel's troops, whom you curse and mock. This very day God is handing you over to me.... The whole earth will know that there's an extraordinary God in Israel. And everyone gathered here will learn that God doesn't save by means of sword or spear. The battle belongs to God."* 1 Samuel 17:22-50 (The Message)

David killed the giant Goliath with just one stone. It went into the one spot on the giant which was not protected—his forehead. David trusted both God's faithfulness and the laws of nature. Have you ever wondered why he picked up his stones from the stream's bed and not just from the side of a hill? He trusted God but also considered physical laws when choosing the stones. Why did David pick up five stones instead of just one? Perhaps he trusted in God's faithfulness but was also planning ahead, knowing that he would have time for five attempts before being killed by Goliath. We will look at what science teaches us about trust and planning in the physical world.

Science Facts: Understanding Aerodynamics

Aerodynamics is the science of objects moving in fluids (water, air, gas). Its laws are used to enable the flight of heavier-than-air objects, like planes. Any object that is thrust into the air will experience three types of forces; lift, drag, and force of gravity. Drag is the friction force on an object flying in the air that tends to slow it down. The drag or resistance that the moving object experiences depends on how blunt or how smooth it is. The more streamlined the object, the further it will travel.

Ornithopter and creator
George White, 1927

The second force is lift. It is the force that holds up an airplane and allows it to fly in the air. For lift to be effective, the object has to have a special shape called airfoil. It should have a smooth surface and travel at a high speed to counter the drag caused by friction. This is why a flying airplane, although much heavier than air, does not fall from the sky. The third force, gravity, tends to pull to earth all objects that are heavier than air.

Birds take advantage of lift force by spreading their wings and flapping them in a manner to reduce drag and maximize lift. When men first tried to imitate birds, they did not understand the laws that govern heavier-than-air flight, and built artificial flapping wings. When they tried to fly, however, the material used for wings was too heavy, the flapping was too energy intensive, and the weight and body shape of the person increased the drag. These inventions were later replaced with fixed winged craft driven by engines. People finally discovered that flight was impossible under human power alone. In early aircraft, engines powered specially designed propellers that accelerated the flow of air over the wings. Later these were replaced by jet engines that created a much higher thrust, which in turn increased the carrying capacity of the airplane, allowing

Boeing 747

it to carry much heavier loads.Examples of these jet airplanes are the well-known Boeing airplanes (737, 747, 757, 767, etc). These airplanes can carry hundreds of passengers at one time with an overall weigh in excess of 200,000 pounds.

In 1903, the Wright brothers were the first to build and test a small, heavier-than-air machine that could fly a few minutes at a time. They could have never imagined that someday huge jet airplanes would carry loads hundreds of thousands of pounds and fly for thousands of miles!

The Wright Brothers and their "Wright Flyer,"
December 17, 1903 at Kitty Hawk, North Carolina

Insights from God's Two Books

When we board an airplane, we often feel a bit worried because it doesn't make sense that this extremely heavy object with all these heavy people in it can stay up in the air. Won't it fall from the sky just like a ball or a rock that has been thrown? When we sit down and begin our trip, we must trust in the laws of aerodynamics to keep our plane airborne. We also trust the pilot to make good decisions based on his training and experience.

In the same way, as we travel through life many things don't make sense. Sometimes bad things happen or we get disappointed with other people. But it is important to trust in Jesus Christ, especially when we are hurt or confused, because he loves us and only wants the best for us—even though his best for us may be different that what we think it should be. Trusting in God's goodness and his love is basic to living the Christian life.

Going back to the story of David and Goliath, remember that David trusted both the laws of nature and God's faithfulness. David trusted God—but he also thought about the physical world when he considered choosing the stones. So trusting God does not mean that we sit back and do nothing. We also have to make wise decisions based on God's word, our experience and our understanding.

Our job:

1 Samuel 17:40 says, *"Then he (David) took his staff in his hand, chose five smooth stones from the stream, put them in his shepherd's bag and, with his sling in his hand, approached the Philistine."* Why did he choose stones from a stream bed rather than picking them up off the ground around him? Answer: They have to be both smooth and dense or heavy. Both friction and weight are important in choosing a projectile. Stones at the bottom of a stream are smooth and heavy because running water makes stones very smooth and heavier stones fall to the bottom of a stream, instead of being carried away by the current. A steel ball or a smooth stone picked from a river bed will go much further and do much more damage than a lighter stone with rough edges. Also, when the object that is thrown rotates—such as a baseball—it creates some lift, and depending on the direction of rotation, it can go slightly up or slightly down. This is how a pitcher can confuse a baseball batter.

God's job:

Why do you think David picked five stones? If he trusted God shouldn't he have picked only one stone? Answer: Perhaps because he was both trusting God and planning. He probably figured he would have about five chances to release a stone before coming within reach of Goliath's sword. So David prepared himself for the situation, but ultimately it was God's intervention that saved the day. David was praised for his deed, but the God of Israel was praised by the people, and even the enemies of Israel realized that he was a mighty God.

Fun with Science

Projectiles: testing the launch angle. Use compressed air squirt guns to test angles of launch and maximum range.

Supplies:

- Compressed air squirt guns
- Water
- Poster board
- Protractor
- Ruler
- Markers

1. Find a large area where you can mark off distances.

2. Use poster board, protractor and ruler to sketch launch angles ranging from 0° (fully horizontal) to 90° (fully vertical). Draw angles at increments of 5 or 10°.

3. Test your squirt gun at each angle. Have a friend mark off the where each shot lands. Which launch angle resulted in the maximum squirting range?

Projectiles: testing the weight and texture of the ammunition. Create marshmallow/water balloon slingshots and test which type of ammunition goes farthest.

Supplies:

- Large funnel (auto parts store or Wal-Mart)
- Extra large rubber bands (can be purchased at office supply stores) or surgical tubing (if you want your projectiles to go *really* far—can be purchased at medical supply stores)
- String
- Small metal washers
- Ammunition (cotton balls, crumpled paper, marshmallows, water balloons, any other objects of varying weight and textures that you would like to test)

1. Drill four holes on *exact opposite* sides of the funnel, two on each side. Mark your drilling sites first because you want to make sure that each hole is directly opposite from the hole on the other side—otherwise your slingshot will be lopsided. Drill them close to the edge of the funnel (not in the middle).

2. Feed the long rubber bands (or surgical tubing) through holes in the funnel and knot them *tightly*. Make sure that each section of tubing makes a large loop. These are the two sides of your slingshot

3. Tie a washer to one end of a short piece of string and feed it through the funnel, then tie a washer on the other end. This is what you will use to grip the launcher so it does not slip through your hand.

4. You have your slingshot! But now it requires teamwork. Have two friends hold a rubber band (or tubing) on each side of the funnel. Load the funnel with ammunition and then, holding the string with the washer, back up—then release and watch the ammunition fly!

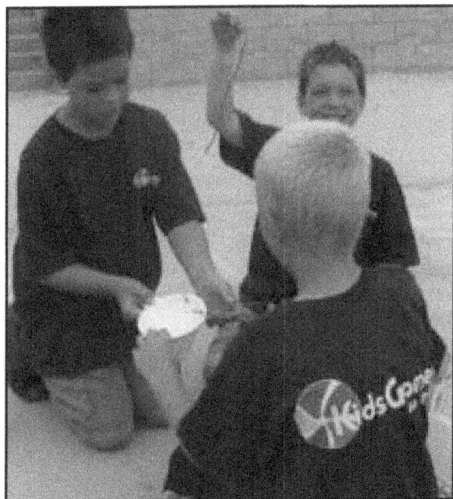

5. Test all types of ammunition, starting with the roughest and lightest. Which type goes highest? Furthest? Test various launch angles—do they match up with your squirt gun results?

I am Created to Obey God

*"God will be a sure foundation for your times, a rich store of salvation
and wisdom and knowledge; the fear of the Lord
is the key to this treasure."*

Isaiah 33:6

Today many people don't want to be told that there are boundaries they must not cross and laws they must obey. Modern people like to do things their own way and follow their own path. This is especially true in Western society, where each person is considered independent, able to make his or her own choices, set their own goals, and 'do their own thing.'

When God created people, however, he also provided a "maintenance manual" to go with his creation. It is called the Bible. It gives us guidelines to help us maintain a life of joy, peace and purpose. The Bible is the story of God loving and seeking his own creation (us) when we so easily try to run away from him. God has given us his Word, not to restrict us and make our lives miserable, but to show us the way to have a wonderful and abundant life. God wants us to have wisdom and understanding. Satan is the one that tries to convince us that God's Way is a way of deprivation and sorrow. The very first question asked in the Bible is found in Genesis 3:1 *"Did God really say, "You must not eat from any tree in the garden?"* Satan wanted Adam and Eve to question God's goodness and convinced them that God was really keeping the best from them. They succumbed to Satan's temptation, which resulted in spiritual and physical death and the entry of evil into the world.

"The fear of the Lord is the beginning of wisdom." (Proverbs 1:7, 9:10, 10:27, 14:27, 19:23) What does this mean? Are we

supposed to live in a constant state of fear? Are we supposed to bring 'offerings' to God so he won't be angry with us? NO! To 'fear the Lord' means to be always aware that I am in the presence of a holy and just God, and that every thought, word and action is open to Him and is being judged by Him. It means to submit to God's rule or lordship over my life, knowing that he is a loving Father and even in difficult times, will be with me and give me strength.

In northern regions lakes and rivers freeze during the winter and are used for ice skating. A skating area needs to be prepared, to make the ice smooth and also to test the ice to make sure it is thick enough. There are usually boundary markers indicating where it is safe to skate. If you go outside these boundaries, you risk breaking through the ice and falling into the frigid water. The boundary markers are there not to restrict people's skating but to free them from having to worry about sinking. In the same way, the Bible gives us laws for living, not to restrict our freedom but to increase it.

Everyone is limited and must live within boundaries. Boundaries can either make you safer and give you freedom to be creative, or become as restrictive as prison walls. Many people are caught in a web of lies and/or bad behaviors. Probably the worst boundary is the prison of addiction. People who are addicted are not free. People who can't control their anger are not free. People who believe they are worthless are not free. In contrast, submitting to God does not limit your freedom but gives you greater freedom.

During the trial before the crucifixion of Jesus, Pilate was frustrated by the lack of response from Jesus and said, *"Don't you realize I have power either to free you or to crucify you?"* Pilate thought that it was he who was 'drawing the boundaries.' Jesus answered, *"You would have no power over me if it were not given to you from above."* (John 19:10, 11) Jesus exposed a much larger perspective, showing that the 'power' Pilate thought he had was simply granted or loaned to him. Jesus on the other hand was truly free. Jesus freely chose to die. He is the only person who ever walked on earth who had the freedom to make that choice, since everyone else is destined to die. By obeying God the Father, he broke all kinds of boundaries, including death, and set us free from sin and eternal separation from God.

What is the difference between a river and a swamp?
Boundaries!

Science Facts: Understanding Boundaries in Nature

The laws that govern the physical world around us set up all types of boundaries in which we have to operate. Without these laws it would be impossible for humans to exist. One such law is the law of gravity that keeps us and everything else firmly on the ground. It also keeps the very air we breathe attached to planet earth. The moon's gravity is very weak. As a result it has no atmosphere and therefore no living things. If the force of gravity on earth were to be 10% stronger, it would retain gases like methane and ammonia in the air, which are poisonous to animal life. If the force of gravity on earth were to be 10%

weaker, the earth would eventually lose all its water into space as vapor. This is one example of how the universe and our solar system are exquisitely fine tuned to permit life to exist as we know it.

If we decide to violate the law of gravity by walking off a tall building, we will fall and hurt ourselves. Thus, the law of gravity places certain boundaries on our movements. However, there is another and counter-acting law called the law of lift and drag, which can counteract gravity for certain objects in flight such as birds, airplanes, etc. This is further described in Section II, Chapter 4.

In 1687 Isaac Newton published a famous book called *Principia,* where he described the law of gravity. He discovered the force that caused physical bodies to attract each other—gravity. He also discovered that this law was universal throughout the universe. [Einstein modified this for extremely high gravitational pulls, like black holes, which is called the General Law of Relativity.] The motions of physical bodies are limited by the amount of the pull of gravity on them. Newton's formula for this gravitational force is: $G \times m_1 \times m_2 / r^2$ (the Inverse Square Law), where m_1 = mass of one body, m_2 = mass of a second body, and r = the distance between the two bodies. G = a universal constant. Tradition says that Newton began thinking about this when he observed apples falling from a tree. This is a common sight, but Newton was an uncommon person who questioned everything and sought to understand the world around him.

Another example of boundaries is our nervous system which is sensitive to pain. As soon as we touch a very hot plate or cut ourselves, the pain nerves signal danger and stop us from damaging our bodies. In one sense, they provide a 'boundary' beyond which we may not go if we do not want to cause ourselves irreparable damage and pain.

A third example has to do with the mathematical modeling of a physical problem. The solution of every such modeling problem requires specifying clear boundary conditions, within which the problem is solved and checked against experimental data. Without boundary conditions, these problems cannot be solved!

Insights from God's Two Books

The Bible uses the eagle as an example of living within and beyond boundaries. *"Those who wait upon God get fresh strength. They spread their wings and soar like eagles. They run and don't get tired, they walk and don't lag behind."* (Isaiah 40:31, The Message).

The eagle is bound by the law of gravity, just like everythin that is heavier than air. If it jumped from a cliff, without opening its wings, it would fall like a rock. But the eagle utilizes another law—the law of lift and drag (aerodynamics). When it spreads its wings another law takes effect, overcoming the law of gravity.

In our lives, the law of gravity is like the law of sin. Our sinful nature causes us to do things we know are wrong. It pulls us down. But when we 'spread our wings' and go forward trusting and obeying God, he helps us overcome the downward pull of sin. *"A new power is in operation. The Spirit of life in Christ, like a strong wind, has magnificently cleared the air, freeing you from a fated lifetime of brutal tyranny at the hands of sin and death."* (Romans 8:2, The Message)

It is scary to trust God, when you might fall off a cliff. When an eagle sees that its young are ready to learn to fly, it gently pushes them out of the nest. Since they don't know how to fly yet, they plunge downward. But the eagle swoops down beneath the eaglet, catches it on its back, then brings it safely back to the nest. This happens several times before the eaglet learns to fly. Deuteronomy 32:11 describes this same process as the way God trains his people to learn to trust in Him. *"God was like an eagle hovering over its nest, overshadowing its young, then spreading its wings, lifting them into the air, teaching them to fly."* (The Message) God trains us to mount up on eagle's wings. Sometimes he stirs up the nest by bringing difficult things into our life. You may feel like you are falling; but he is underneath ready to catch you. God only asks you to grow deeper in him and allow him to carry you above the turbulence into the higher air currents where there is rest.

Fun with Science

Demonstration of Overcoming Gravity

Centrifugal Force

Tie a weight to a string. See that it immediately falls down.

Hold the end of the string and swing the weight in a circle. Note that the weight rises up and no longer hangs down. It is now under the influence of another law—the Law of Centripetal/Centrifugal Force.

Bernoulli's Principle

Daniel Bernoulli, an 18th century mathematician, discovered an amazing thing about moving air, and it is this principal that allows heavy objects, like airplanes, to fly.

Bernoulli's principle: as the velocity of a fluid increases, the pressure exerted by that fluid decreases (the faster air flows over an object, the less the air pushes on it). As airplanes move, the air rushing over the wings exerts less pressure than the air under the wings. That greater pressure under the wings provides the lift that forces the plane upward.

You can easily illustrate this principle by using a simple note card. Bend it lengthwise so that it makes an arched shape, and then place it on a table. Now, blow under the card and see if you can overturn it. Not as easy as it looks! It starts clinging, rather than rising. This is because the air stream (moving air) produces a lower pressure *under* the card, so the normal air pressure above the card presses it into the table.

Another fun demonstration of *Bernoulli's Principle* is the famous floating ping-pong ball experiment.

Supplies:

- o   Hair dryer
- o   Ping pong ball
- o   Toilet paper tube

1.   Use the cool setting on the hair dryer. Turn it on and point it at the ceiling.

2. Place the ping pong ball above the hair dryer and see if you can float it in the air stream. What happens if you move around? (*Gravity pulls down on the ball—but the air stream from the hair dryer pushes it up. These forces are balanced, and the ball should hover in mid-air. When you move around the ball is forced out of the flowing airstream, into the relatively high pressure air around it. This high pressure should push the ball back into the lower pressure flowing airstream—so it should float no matter how much you move around.*)

3. Place the toilet paper tube in the air above the ball—can you get the ping pong ball to be sucked up into the tube? Why do you think the ball is sucked up into the tube? (*The air is funneled into an even smaller area, making it rush through faster and thus lower the pressure even more.*)

4. Test other light weight objects (balloons, beach balls, etc.). Try two or more balls. What happens? How many can you float at once? How do they behave when there is more than one object?

5. Now try levitating a ball in the corner of the room. What happens when there are walls on two sides?

139

I am Created for a Purpose

'It's in Christ that we find out who we are and what we are living for. Long before we first heard of Christ and got our hopes up, he had his eye on us, had designs on us for glorious living, part of the overall purpose he is working out in everything and everyone."

Ephesians 1:11 (The Message)

Many educated people believe that everything can be explained in terms of natural causes and laws, without the need for moral, spiritual, or supernatural explanations. People who believe this are called 'naturalists.' According to naturalists, man is the most advanced form in the animal world, having evolved through the evolutionary chain, and whose existence and behavior can be explained by the laws of matter and energy. One of the biggest problems with this naturalistic belief system is having to deal with the issue of purpose. People have a great need to feel that their life has purpose. It can be depressing to learn that you are simply an 'accident', that your life has no purpose, and when you die, that will be the end. Even naturalists live as if their lives have purpose, as many are seeking to advance knowledge and understanding in many academic fields.

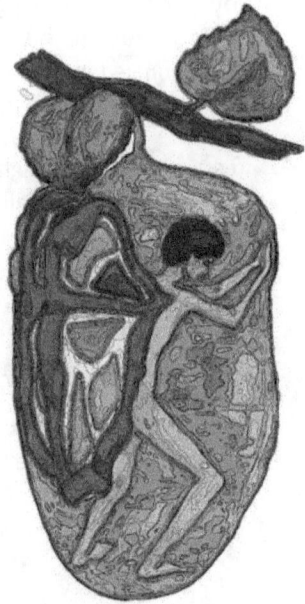

In contrast to the naturalistic approach, meaning and purpose are at the core of God's creation as expressed in the Bible. God gave Adam a purpose right after he created him: name the animals and tend the garden. God has a purpose in all he does. In Isaiah 46:9-11 God declares: *"I am God and there is no other; I say: My purpose will stand, and I will do all that I please… what I have planned, that will I do."* Apostle Paul writes: *"All things God works for the good of those who love him, who have been called according to his purpose."* (Romans 8:28) So those who belong to God are created for a very noble and high purpose, a purpose that will continue into eternity. They are to become like Jesus Christ and to work in the Kingdom of God. Many times it is difficult to understand the purpose God has called us to, but as we walk with God, his purpose for our lives becomes clearer.

As a young man, Joseph (Genesis 37-47) was given a vision of God's purpose for him. The dream involved his older brothers bowing down to him. His brothers hated him for this and also because their father, Jacob, loved Joseph more than any of the other children. When an opportunity came to get rid of Joseph, the brothers sold him into slavery in Egypt, and told their father that an animal had killed and eaten him. For about 12 years Joseph suffered in Egypt, serving as a slave and then being put in jail. During all this time, Joseph was faithful to God and in the end, God honored his faithfulness and did put Joseph in a high position in Egypt, second-in-command under Pharaoh. When there was a famine in the land where Joseph's brothers lived, they had to come to Egypt seeking food. There they met Joseph and did bow down to him, just as God had predicted in the dream. Joseph, however, was not angry with them or with God because of all the suffering he endured. Instead, he said, *"Do not be distressed and do not be angry with yourselves for selling me here, because it was to save lives that God sent me ahead of you…It was not you who sent me here, but God."* (Genesis 45:5 and 8)

Our lives have great meaning and significance. God who *"brings out the starry host one by one and calls them each by name"* (Isaiah 40:26), also calls us by name, even knowing how many hairs are on our head. (Matt. 10:30) God also gives us purpose, calling us to work along with him in his kingdom.

Science Facts: Understanding Purpose in Nature

Not only do we observe design in nature from the living cell to the vast universe, we also detect purposeful activities in all living organisms, from the smallest microbe, to insects, animals and of course, human beings. Among the many amazing behaviors of insects, an outstanding example is the awesome sight of the seasonal mass migration of the monarch butterfly. These small creatures, weighing about one gram, fly each fall from the northern United States and southern Canada to their wintering grounds in Central Mexico, a distance of over 2,000 miles! They are able to accomplish this amazing feat by following the sun and using a circadian clock, which is a time-compensated clock located in the antennae of the butterfly. This clock calculates seasonal migration routes relative to the sun's position (Reference 8). All this is done in a brain that is the size of a pin head!

Two features of the monarch butterfly help protect it from predators (birds, frogs, mice and lizards). First, the larva or caterpillar feeds on the milkweed plant which contains the toxic chemical glycosides. This is poisonous to the predators. Farmers consider the monarch a beneficial insect because the milkweed is a noxious plant that invades some farms and the caterpillar helps to control it. Secondly, when the predator sees the distinctive orange colored wings of the monarch butterfly with their brown or black edges and white spots, it avoids eating the insect, thus allowing the butterfly to travel those long distances without getting killed.

Monarch butterflies go through four stages: egg, larva (caterpillar), chrysalis, and adult butterfly. Only the third or fourth generation lives long enough to travel to warmer climates, hibernate and then in the spring lay the eggs that begin the cycle again. When the millions of monarch butterflies from all over the northern latitudes arrive in central Mexico at the beginning of winter, they land on trees in a forest the size of a few city blocks. There they hibernate during the cold months and in the spring the female lays its eggs and that generation dies. The new generation of butterflies hatch, become larvae and eventually change into butterflies and fly back north. They reproduce and die, usually in the Southern United States. The next generation moves a bit further north. Finally, the third or fourth generation is born and instead of living only two months, it lives seven or eight months. This makes it possible for the monarch to fly to its northern limits and then reverse course and fly south for the winter, arriving in the exact spot where its 'great grandparents' came from!

Science Trivia: How can you tell a male Monarch from a female?

Answer: *The male monarch has a black spot in the center of each of its hind wings over a vein. The female does not have this spot and its veins are wider and darker.*

More information can be found on Wikipedia and also at: www.monarch-butterfly.com

Insights from God's Two Books

Looking at the Monarch Butterfly we can learn much about living a life of purpose.

1. Cocoon stage—a time of preparation;

2. Nourishment—the Word of God protects you from enemies, like the milkweed protects the butterfly from predators;

3. Three lives / one direction—Each butterfly participates in the process and each is important (We are the body of Christ);

4. Oriented toward the sun—"Keep your eyes on Jesus, who both began and finished this race we're in. Study how he did it. Because he never lost sight of where he was headed." Hebrews 12:2 (The Message).

Today people misuse the Theory of Evolution to imply that our lives have no purpose, they are simply the outcome of chance happenings. However, even scientists who claim there is no purpose in life, act purposefully. They live expecting a good outcome for their work. They justify their science by stating that it will help make life better for people by controlling things such as viruses, bacteria, droughts, genetic disorders, etc. It is impossible to live a healthy life without purpose. That is how God made us. Great joy comes from finding your purpose, or 'marching orders' from God and fulfilling them.

Fun with Science

What about growing your own butterflies?

- http://www.butterfly-gifts.com/

- http://www.amazon.com/Insect-Lore-Live-Butterfly-Pavillion/
dp/B00004U5UF

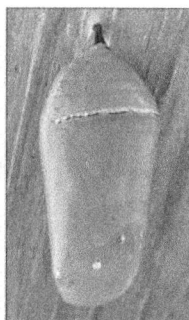

The male monarch: note the small matching black spots toward the center of the lower wing.

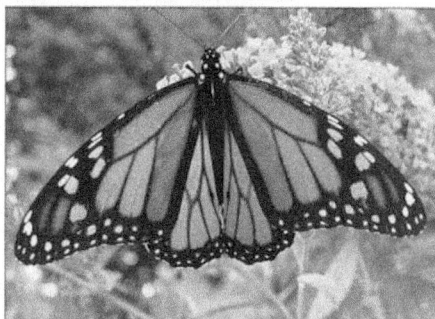

Part III

How Do I Follow Jesus?

Seeking Treasure

"Seek first his kingdom and his righteousness and all these things (food and clothing) will be given to you as well."
Matthew 6:33

A famous parable told by Jesus is called "The Prodigal Son." This story is about a young man who grew up in a wealthy home, but was not content with his life and wanted to go his own way. He boldly asked his father to divide the inheritance between his brother and himself, and to give him the portion due him, even though his father had not yet died. Amazingly, the father did what his son asked, and the son left home with a small fortune in his pocket. In his travels he wasted everything his father had given him and ended up broke. *"There was a bad famine all through that country and he began to hurt. He signed on with a citizen there who assigned him to his fields to slop the pigs. He was so hungry he would have eaten the corncobs in the pig slop, but no one would give him any. That brought him to his senses. He said, 'All those farmhands working for my father sit down to three meals a day, and here I am starving to death. I'm going back to my father. I'll say to him, Father, I've sinned against God, I've sinned before you; I don't deserve to be called your son. Take me on as a hired hand.' He got right up and went home to his father.*

*When he was still a long way off, his father saw him. His heart
pounding, he ran out, embraced him, and kissed him. The son started
his speech: 'Father, I've sinned against God, I've sinned before you; I
don't deserve to be called your son ever again.' But the father wasn't
listening. He was calling to the servants, 'Quick. Bring a clean set of
clothes and dress him. Put the family ring on his finger and sandals on
his feet. Then get a grain-fed heifer and roast it. We're going to feast!
We're going to have a wonderful time! My son is here—given up for
dead and now alive! Given up for lost and now found!"* (Luke
15:14-24, The Message)

This young man learned the hard way that seeking treasure
apart from the Father led to poverty, both physical poverty and
poverty of spirit. The Bible speaks a lot about seeking real
treasure, treasure that will last. The world tells us that our lives
are all about getting stuff, and more stuff, and if not stuff, at
least getting fame and power. Jesus told another parable about a
man who did just that.

*"The farm of a certain rich man produced a terrific crop. He talked
to himself: 'What can I do? My barn isn't big enough for this harvest.'
Then he said, 'Here's what I'll do: I'll tear down my barns and build
bigger ones. Then I'll gather in all my grain and goods, and I'll say to
myself, Self, you've done well! You've got it made and can now retire.
Take it easy and have the time of your life!" "Just then God showed up
and said, 'Fool! Tonight you die. And your barnful of goods—who gets
it?'*

*"That's what happens when you fill your barn with Self and not
with God."*

*Steep yourself in God-reality, God-initiative, God-provisions.
You'll find all your everyday human concerns will be met. Don't be
afraid of missing out. You're my dearest friends! The Father wants to
give you the very kingdom itself. Be generous. Give to the poor. Get
yourselves a bank that can't go bankrupt, a bank in heaven far from
bank robbers, safe from embezzlers, a bank you can bank on. It's*

obvious, isn't it? The place where your treasure is, is the place you will most want to be, and end up being." Luke 12:16-21, (The Message)

Science Facts: Understanding the Scientific Method

A good definition of the **Scientific Method** given by the American Association for the Advancement of Science (AAAS) can be stated as follows:

It is a way of knowing based upon testable descriptions of the world obtained through human interpretation in natural categories of publicly observable and reproducible sense data (information obtained through our five senses), obtained by interaction with the natural world. (Reference 9)

It should be noted that the above definition is based on several assumptions. These are:

1. Physical reality exists and is objectively observable

2. Logic applies in scientific descriptions of reality

3. Some cause and effect operates in reality

The steps of the Scientific Method are to:

1. Observe a phenomena

2. Ask questions

3. Do careful research

4. Construct a hypothesis

5. Test the hypothesis by experimentation and/or observation

6. Analyze the data and draw conclusions

7. Share your results with the scientific community

8. Modify your conclusions as necessary

The Scientific Method can be applied to:

1. **Empirical Data:** based on direct or indirect observations, repeated experimentation, and laboratory verification.

2. **Observational data:** based on contemporary observations such as in Astrophysics, where direct testing is not available but verification can be established by laboratory simulation.

3. **Historical Information:** based on recorded data (often incomplete) from the past, such as archaeology and geology. In this case there is no possibility of laboratory verification. Conclusions often require inference to the best explanation.

Insights from God's Two Books

The manner with which the scientific method works tracks closely the searching process mentioned in the Bible. *"You will seek me and find me when you seek me with all your heart."* (Jeremiah 29:13). A scientist observes nature and starts by asking a question: What causes this to happen? What are the laws behind this particular phenomenon? Next she starts seeking answers to the question by formulating a hypothesis, conducting tests, and improving or correcting her original hypothesis. She continues experimenting and testing until a theory emerges that best explains the phenomena being observed. When she succeeds, it is as if a door has been opened for her to better see and understand the wonders of nature. In the same way, God says that truth will be revealed to those who seek diligently and with perseverance. The scientist who succeeds 'asks and seeks' with a focused passion, not giving up until the 'door opens.' In fact, the one who eventually wins the Nobel Prize is the determined person who throws all his energy behind the search for discovering a scientific 'treasure.'

Once a law is discovered and formulated, it applies everywhere. It is universal and can be verified by other scientists and is applicable throughout the cosmos. There is no such thing as a 'personal truth' in science, where something is true for one person but not true for another. In the same way, the Bible states that truth comes from God, is unchanging and universal. Jesus himself said that he is "the truth."

Fun with Science (Scientific Method)

Empirical Data

Make a pendulum using strings of different lengths and weights of different materials, which you will attach to the string at one end. Use one string (same length) with the different weights and measure the period. A period is the time it takes to complete a whole swing back and forth. You will need a stop watch to measure the time. Then change the length of the string and measure the periods again.

Which of these two factors will change the period of the pendulum—the length of the string or the weight at the end of the string?

Observational Data

Compare the motion of the planets and stars. Make a note of the positions of several stars and planets in your night sky.

Observe their relative motion over a period of several nights. Determine which heavenly bodies remain in place and which move. Look up the origin of the word 'planet.' How is it appropriate to your observations?

Historical Observation

Look at the historical record of original documents written by various famous ancient authors listed below. Notice when the original documents were written and then the time span between those original documents and the earliest copies that have been found. Just using the method of Historical Observation which document would you say is most reliable or closest to the original? (Reference 10)

Manuscript Evidence of the New Testament Compared to Written Works of Antiquity

Author	When Written	Earliest Copy	Time Span	# of Copies
Plato (*Tetralogics*)	427-347 B.C.	900 A.D.	1,200 yrs.	7
Tactitus (*Annals*)	100 B.C.	100 A.D.	200 yrs.	20
Thucydides (*History*)	460-400 B.C.	900 A.D.	1,300 yrs.	8
Herodotus (*History*)	480-425 B.C.	900 A.D.	1,300 yrs.	8
Sophocles	496-406 B.C.	1000 A.D.	1,400 yrs.	100
Aristotle	384-322 B.C.	1100 A.D.	1,400 yrs.	5
The Four Gospels	45-90 A.D.	300-450 A.D.	250 yrs.	24,970

Fun with Science

Here is a classic, simple experiment that uses the scientific method.

Supplies:
- ○ Dirty pennies
- ○ Ketchup or taco sauce (Taco Bell taco sauce works well)
- ○ Toothpicks and Q-Tips
- ○ Tomato paste
- ○ Salt
- ○ Vinegar

- • **Observe a Phenomena**: Use a toothpick to make a pattern on a dirty penny with dabs of ketchup or taco sauce. Wait at least minute, then wipe off the ketchup with the paper towel. *What do you see?*

- • **Ask Questions:** Why is the penny dirty? What has happened to the penny? Why?

- • **Do Research:** Find out why pennies get dirty. Read up on the ingredients in ketchup or taco sauce.

- • **Construct a Hypothesis:** What or which components might be responsible for the cleaning power of ketchup or taco sauce?

- • **Test the Hypothesis:** Collect all the ingredients you want to test: tomato paste, salt, vinegar, anything else you want to test. Collect a bunch of dirty pennies and arrange them on a paper grid so that you can label each test. Label one penny as the control (no ingredients added) and label one penny for each single ingredient (salt, tomato paste, vinegar, etc.). Cover the pennies with the various ingredients (using q-tips) and allow them to sit for a few minutes.

- • **Analyze the Data and Make Conclusions:** Rinse the pennies with water (be careful to keep track of which penny is which) and write down your observations. Which of these ingredients did a good job of cleaning the dirty pennies?

- • **Share and Modify Conclusions:** Think about what you could try next—how about combinations of ingredients?

Now label a penny for each combination: (salt and vinegar, tomato paste and vinegar, salt and tomato paste, etc.). Once again cover the pennies with the various ingredients (using q-tips) and allow them to sit for a few minutes.

- **Re-Analyze the Data and Make New Conclusions:** What is the final result? Which ingredient or combination of ingredients worked best to remove the tarnish from pennies?

Some explanation of the results!

The Household Chemistry of Cleaning Pennies, *J. Chem. Educ.*, 2001, *78* (4), p 513.
(Note: the full article must be obtained through subscription or library)
http://pubs.acs.org/doi/abs/10.1021/ed078p513

Or, for a simpler discussion:
http://www.cruftbox.com/cruft/docs/cleaningcopper.html

Science Trivia: Who was the famous Russian scientist that set back the biological sciences in the Soviet Union by using the scientific method inappropriately. His scientific ineptness led to a funny story. A scientist took a flea, put him on his hand and asked the flea to jump. The flea jumped. The scientist then cut off the flea's hind legs and asked him to jump. The flea could not jump. The scientist concluded that if you cut off the hind legs of a flea, it loses its hearing.

Answer: Levchenko

Making Right Choices

*"There is a way that seems right to a man
but in the end it leads to death."*
Proverbs 16:25

The Bible says that whatever you sow, you will also reap. This illustration is based on gardening principles. If you put the seed of a watermelon in the ground, the plant that grows will be a watermelon plant—not a tomato plant or a rose plant. In the same way, the choices we make will have consequences. If we sow good choices, our lives will be productive and blessed. If we make bad choices, our lives will have much sorrow and difficulty. God wants us to make good choices and gives us lots of help in making those choices. The book of Proverbs is dedicated to helping young people gain wisdom. The entire Bible helps us see life from God's perspective which gives us wisdom to make good choices. Just like views of the earth from satellites or from Google Earth, having God's perspective helps us see the bigger picture or the topography (surface features) of the landscape.

Before David became a king, he was a simple shepherd. After the prophet Samuel predicted that he would become king, the ruling king of Israel, King Saul, became jealous and frightened of David. The king's men told King Saul that David was out to overthrow him and that King Saul should kill him while he had a chance. David was in hiding with his friends because he knew that King Saul was searching for him.

One day David and his friends heard that King Saul was very near. They saw a nearby cave and went into it, to the very back of the cave. While they were hiding there, King Saul passed by and wanted to rest a bit so he went into the cave. While he was resting, David snuck up behind him and cut off the corner of his robe. Eventually the king left the cave to join his soldiers and to continue the search for David. When King Saul was a short distance down the road, David came out of the cave holding a piece of the king's robe.

David called to Saul and bowed down and said, "My king! Why do you listen to those who say 'David is out to get you.' This very day with your very own eyes you have seen that just now in the cave God put you in my hands. My men wanted me to kill you, but I wouldn't do it. I told them that I won't lift a finger against my master—he's God's anointed…Look at this piece I cut from your robe. I could have cut you —killed you—but I didn't. Look at the evidence! I'm not against you. I'm no rebel. I haven't sinned against you, and yet you're hunting me down to kill me…God may avenge me, but it is in his hands, not mine."

After Saul heard David, he said "You've heaped good on me; I've dumped evil on you. ..May God give you a bonus of blessings for what you've done for me today! I know now beyond doubt that you will rule as king." (1 Samuel 24, The Message)

David had the choice of becoming king through his own power by killing the living king or waiting on God and letting

God avenge him and give him the throne. David made the right choice when he decided to let God be the judge. *"Trust God from the bottom of your heart; don't try to figure out everything on your own. Listen for God's voice in everything you do, everywhere you go; He's the one who will keep you on track."* (Proverbs 3:5, 6, The Message).

Science Facts: Understanding Magnetism

From the earliest days of mankind, people have needed help in knowing where they were and how to get to someplace else. Early civilizations used the stars and planets to guide them in their travels. Up until the 1300's, seafarers used the stars to navigate across seas and oceans. Then in 1269 a soldier named Peter Peregrinus discovered magnetism, and that the earth had a magnetic field, and this discovery changed the way people traveled.

Naturally occurring magnetism is the property of certain metals which allows them to interact with all types of magnetic fields. A magnetic material will attract other metals with the same properties, or repel them, depending on the polarity. Some metals that best demonstrate magnetic properties are nickel, iron, cobalt and their alloys. You can hold a piece of this magnetized metal in your hand—you would call this your typical "magnet"—but the principle of magnetism works on a *much* larger scale than that. The very core of our planet is, in fact, a magnet. It's made up of metals with magnetic properties, making the entire *earth* act as a huge magnet with two ends (which are near the north and south poles). In other, more scientific terms, the earth has a magnetic field, just like any magnetic object does.

What makes the earth's magnetic field so useful is the fact that any small piece of material that can be magnetized, such as iron, will be affected by that field, and will tend to align itself with the earth's north magnetic pole, meaning that it will point NORTH. Once you know which direction is north, you can determine the other directions and which way to go.

A compass is a tool that helps people know the direction in which they are traveling. It has a freely moveable pointer that is magnetized, usually pointing toward the earth's magnetic north pole. The other cardinal points (south, west, east) are indicated as well. The compass is an invaluable tool for travelers, particularly those on large bodies of water, where there are no landmarks.

A modern day navigational tool is the Global Positioning System (GPS). It was developed by the U.S. Department of Defense and uses satellites that orbit the earth, to transmit microwaves to receivers, which in turn, indicate the location, and often the direction, speed and time of the person or object to which it is attached.

Vast amounts of information are now available to help people know where they are and how to find their way in unfamiliar territory. Much information can be found on topographical maps and from them you can learn a lot about any location. Today we have "bird's eye view" maps of the entire world through Google Earth and can pretend to fly over distant landscapes.

Insights from God's Two Books

God has given each person an internal moral compass. It is called the conscience. Even from a young age, your conscience will let you know when you have done something wrong. The problem is that we don't like to pay attention to our conscience because we want to do things our way, not God's way. God uses our conscience to speak to us through those in authority over us like parents and other people in our lives, and also through the Bible. When we don't listen to our conscience it slowly gets weaker and weaker, until we hardly hear it at all. When that happens we can really lose our way in life and make many bad choices.

Life is like a journey. Sometimes the landscape is wonderful, full of trees, brooks, meadows and beauty. Sometimes the landscape gets rough with deep gorges, freezing blizzards or deep rivers to cross, and that is especially when we need to depend on God and listen to him. David had to go through many rough times before he became king of Israel, but he always listened to God and trusted him. Most of the Psalms were written by David, and from them we can see that he had a close relationship with God and loved God very much.

A famous French physicist and philosopher, Blaise Pascal (1623-1662), said *"There is a God-shaped vacuum in the heart of every man which cannot be filled by any created thing, but only by God, the Creator, made known through Jesus."* So when we focus our lives on loving God and fill our hearts with his Word, we are strengthening our inner compass. This will help us as we make decisions because God promises to "lead us in the good way" when we trust in him; otherwise we will certainly make bad choices. *"There is a way that seems right to a man but in the end it leads to death."* (Proverbs 16:25) Although God still forgives us when we make bad choices, we will have to pay the consequences. *"Don't be misled: No one makes a fool of God. What a person plants, he will harvest. The person who plants selfishness, ignoring the needs of others—ignoring God!—harvests a crop of weeds…But the one who plants in response to God, letting God's Spirit do the growth work in him, harvests a crop of real life, eternal life."* (Galatians 6: 7-8; The Message)

Fun with Science

Experiment with magnets

Supplies:

- o N-S magnets
- o Fe (iron) filings
- o Paper plates (thin)
- o Collect all sorts of items, metallic and non-metallic

Pour Fe (iron) filings onto thin paper plates. Hold the N-S magnets below the plate and see if you can create and visualize the north and south magnetic fields.

The high permeability of individual iron filings causes the magnetic field to be larger at the end of the filings. This causes individual filings to attract each other, forming elongated clusters that trace out the appearance of lines.

Then test your magnets on different items to find out which are magnetic and which are not.

Using a Compass

Experience for yourself the process of navigating by compass. Have an adult or friend hide something and set up a simple "route" or map for you to follow to get to it.

Using a compass along with a MAP

Take your navigational skills to the next level—use a compass to orient yourself on a map.

Using Google Earth

Go to Google Earth on your computer and locate the En Gedi wilderness, where David hid in the cave. It is located south of Jericho, along the west bank of the Dead Sea.

Growing in Wisdom

"And Jesus grew in wisdom and stature,
and in favor with God and men."

Luke 2:52

Sometimes when we make decisions, the choice is clearly between right and wrong. But most of the time, our choices are made based on whether we are walking in the way of wisdom or the way of foolishness. The Book of Proverbs was written to teach young people how to walk in the way of wisdom and avoid the way of foolishness. God wants us to walk in wisdom and reap the benefits of a life well-lived.

King Solomon is regarded as one of the wisest men who ever lived and most of the wise sayings in the Book of Proverbs are his. After becoming King of Israel, he went before the altar of the Lord and offered a thousand burnt offerings. God was pleased with his offerings and said, *"Ask for whatever you want me to give you."* Solomon asked for wisdom. *"Give me wisdom and knowledge, that I may lead this people."* God said to Solomon, *"Since this is your heart's desire and you have not asked for wealth, riches or honor...therefore wisdom and knowledge will be given you. And I will also give you wealth, riches and honor, such as no king who was before you ever had and none after you will have."* (2 Chronicles 1:10) God was pleased with Solomon's request. In James 1:5 we are also invited to ask for wisdom.

1 Samuel 18-20 tells a wonderful story of two young men who needed wisdom. King Saul was ruling Israel at the time and because of disobedience, God had removed his Spirit from the King who was becoming more and more wicked. David was

a young man and God's Spirit rested on him. Everything he did turned out great! He was successful in battle, he played music beautifully and many of the girls were in love with him. King Saul was jealous. King Saul had a son, Jonathan, who loved David and the two of them were best friends. Jonathan couldn't believe that his father hated David to the point of wanting to kill him.

It came time to celebrate a national holiday and David was expected to be in attendance, but he was afraid that the king would try to kill him at the party; so he and Jonathan worked out a plan. Jonathan would attend the party and talk to his dad, to see if he was indeed trying to kill David. David would pretend that he had to go visit his family and couldn't attend the party. When Jonathan told his father why David was not in attendance, King Saul became furious and Jonathan realized that he *did* intend to kill David.

David and Jonathan had worked out a secret plan of communication. Jonathan would shoot arrows from a field while David hid behind a boulder. Jonathan would then tell his servant to go pick up the arrows. If he said, "The arrows are on this side," that meant that it was OK for David to come in. If he said, "The arrows are further out," that meant that David was to escape. Jonathan ended up saying to his servant, "Isn't the arrow further out? Hurry, quick, don't just stand there." David escaped, running as fast as he could.

David and Jonathan were wise in their decision. They recognized danger but weren't sure how serious it was. They carefully looked into the situation and then had a plan to deal with whatever the reality was. They were united in their love and respect for one another.

A "Making Wise Choices" Maze

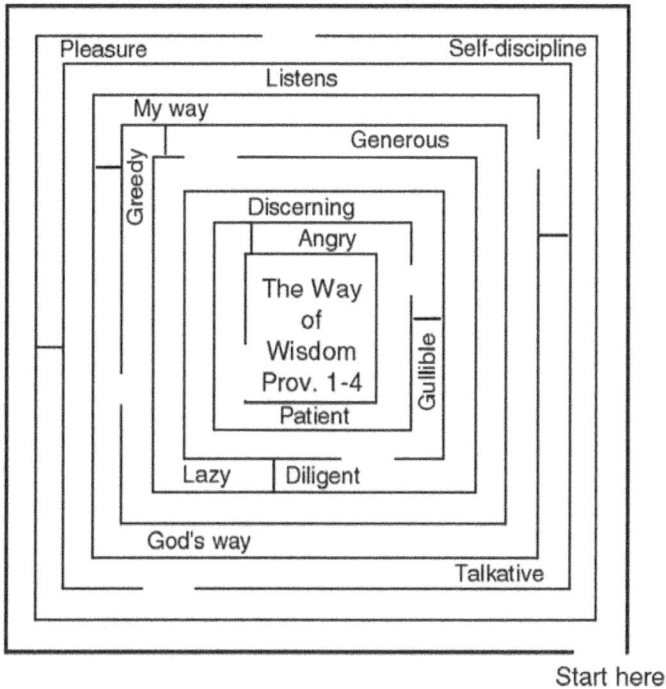

```
Pleasure                        Self-discipline
        Listens
   My way
                        Generous
 Greedy
           Discerning
             Angry
           The Way
              of
            Wisdom      Gullible
            Prov. 1-4
             Patient
     Lazy   | Diligent
   God's way
                              Talkative
```

Start here

Wisdom comes when we are:

1. Humble; willing to learn from others and willing to be corrected.

2. Listening to God and others in authority over us, like parents.

3. Studying and thinking about God's Word. *"I have more insight than all my teachers, for I meditate on your statutes. I have more understanding than the elders, for I obey your precepts."* Psalm 119: 99, 100

4. Seek God. *"Seek first his (the Heavenly Father) kingdom and his righteousness, and all these things will be given to you as well."* (Matthew 6:33)

Science Facts: Understanding Cryptography

Cryptography comes from the Greek word 'kryptos'—meaning hidden or secret; 'grapho'—meaning writing. It is the practice and study of hiding information. The earliest types of encryption (the conversion of readable, understandable material to nonsense) involved simple methods such as replacement of words or rearranging the order of letters according to a key. The purpose was usually to convey an important message without others being able to understand it. The person receiving the message would need to have the 'key' in order to unlock the message. The act of creating secret messages has been around for thousands of years.

One of these ancient secret codes was created by Julius Caesar to send coded military information, and is known as the 'Caesar Cipher.' It was what is known as a 'substitution code,' a code in which a letter is simply replaced with another letter, usually one that is shifted a set position up or down the alphabet. In the Caesar Cipher, each letter is replaced with a letter shifted 3 positions down the alphabet, so that:

A B C D E F G H I J K L M N O P Q R S T U V W X Y Z

becomes:

D E F G H I J K L M N O P Q R S T U V W X Y Z A B C

And a secret message might be (can you figure it out?):

WKH TXLFN EURZQ IRA MXPSV RYHU
WKH ODCB GRJ

During Caesar's time this was an almost unbreakable code, because most people were illiterate and could not even read the alphabet! These days a code like this would be fairly simple to break once you guessed that it is just letter substitution. Nonetheless, if you only looked at the individual pieces of the code, you would never really understand the intended message, simple as it is. A successful code breaker must also 'stand back' and look at the entire scheme or system along with looking at the details. Once you started recognizing patterns in the letters, and how frequently they appear (in any given stretch of written language, certain letters and combinations of letters occur with varying frequencies), you could start to break the code, letter by letter. Without these two perspectives, the detailed and the systemic view, a person would not be very good at understanding the message being communicated.

Of course throughout history, codes have become much more complex. Cryptanalysis (the study of code breaking methods) is much more complicated and there are many techniques you can use to find the keys needed to break hidden codes. Today encoding (encrypting) electronic messages is more important than ever because so much sensitive information is sent over the internet and decryption methods are much more sophisticated.

Cryptography played an important role in World War II as opposing military forces tried to understand the secret messages of their enemies. In Poland there is a memorial (Poznan Monument) to the cryptologists who broke Germany's Enigma Machine's ciphers. This breakthrough played an important role in the Allies defeat of Nazi Germany.

In our digital era, cryptography has moved away from focusing on language toward focusing on mathematics. Very advanced mathematical analysis is now needed in order to practice cryptography. The purpose is not just to send secret messages, but involves large-scale economic transactions and vast transfers of information. Modern day cryptographers are like soldiers fighting a powerful enemy, not with guns and bombs, but with mathematics, engineering and physics.

Science Trivia: Navajo Code Talkers

During World War II the Japanese were very successful at breaking the codes of the U.S. military. This helped the Japanese prepare for attacks because they knew the plans of the enemy. To solve this problem a young man named Philip Johnston, a son of missionaries to the Navajos, proposed to the military that they enlist Navajo men who could transmit messages using their native language. The Navajo language at that time had no alphabet and was extremely difficult to learn. Only about 30 non-natives knew how to speak it.

So the Navajos became 'code talkers' during 1942-1945 and transmitted hundreds of messages. During the first 48 hours of the Battle of Iwo Jima, the Code Talkers transmitted 800 messages. The Japanese were never able to break the code! The Code Talkers would substitute some of their native words for military words, like 'chicken hawk' actually meant 'dive-bomber.' They also assigned Navajo words to correspond to letters in the alphabet. The proud Navajo Code Talkers contributed to the success of the United States in World War II.

Insights from God's Two Books

In the Bible, God urges us to seek wisdom above all else. Wisdom begins with an attitude of respect and honor toward God. God also urges us to get understanding. Although much like wisdom, understanding involves getting the facts right and gaining knowledge, while wisdom comes from having the facts and knowledge, and then being able to look at them from the right perspective. Many people have a lot of knowledge about certain subjects; but very few people are able to use their knowledge to gain wisdom. To be wise, one must be humble before the one who created us and see life from his eternal perspective.

In the same way, those who want to be successful in breaking codes must gain a lot of knowledge about the science of cryptography. In the early days it involved knowing the 'key' to the codes, but today a cryptographer learns about information theory, statistics, abstract algebra, number theory and much more. As cryptography has grown more complex, the perspective has expanded.

God gives us a 'key' to help us understand him and his word. That 'key' is found when we learn to honor, trust and respect him. Wisdom develops as we look deeper and deeper into who God is and what he is telling us through both his written word and the living word, Jesus. A successful cryptographer must look at the entire scheme or system along with looking at the details of the code he is trying to break. Without the two perspectives of looking at the details (numbers and/or letters) as well as looking at the 'bigger picture' (system analysis), a person would not be a very good cryptographer. In the same way, wisdom is the skill of understanding the details of life (knowledge) and at the same time, looking at it from God's perspective.

Fun with Science

Creating your own encrypted codes.

Websites for learning about secret codes and making your own:

- http://www.nsa.gov/kids/home.shtml
- http://www.thunk.com/

Online Morse code machines (not a secret code, but fun to experiment with):

- http://boyslife.org/games/online-games/575/morse-code-machine
- http://www.classbraingames.com/2009/12/learn-morse-code/

Understanding Consequences

"A man reaps what he sows. The one who sows to please his sinful nature, from that nature will reap destruction; the one who sows to please the Spirit, from the Spirit will reap eternal life."

Galatians 6:8

"The way to life—to God—is vigorous and requires total attention...The words I speak to you are not incidental additions to your life, homeowner improvements to your standard of living. They are foundational words, words to build a life on. If you work these words into your life, you are like a smart carpenter who built his house on solid rock. Rain poured down, the river flooded, a tornado hit—but nothing moved that house. It was fixed to the rock.

"But if you just use my words in Bible studies and don't work them into your life, you are like a stupid carpenter who built his house on the sandy beach. Then a storm rolled in and the waves came up, it collapsed like a house of cards." Matthew 7:24—27 (The Message)

After Jesus spoke to the crowd, they stood up and cheered. They knew that Jesus was speaking truth, truth that brings real life, abundant life.

What we think and what we believe have consequences. Our actions always start in our heads, in our thinking. God has created us in his image so our actions are not based primarily on instinct, like the animals. Instead, God has made us so that we are receptive to thoughts, ideas, what other people say and do. God wants to give us his thoughts through his Word and a relationship with him. But the world system also wants to influence our thoughts through things we see on TV or on the internet, or things we hear from friends, teachers or the media. It is up to you to choose which ideas you will allow into your brain. At first this may not seem very important. What difference does it make what TV shows I watch or whether I listen to my parent's advice or not? The real test will come when the "storm" hits. When things go wrong or are confusing, then it will really matter. So what seems small in the beginning can have big consequences in the future. Listen to what Jesus said. Build your house (thoughts and life) on a rock.

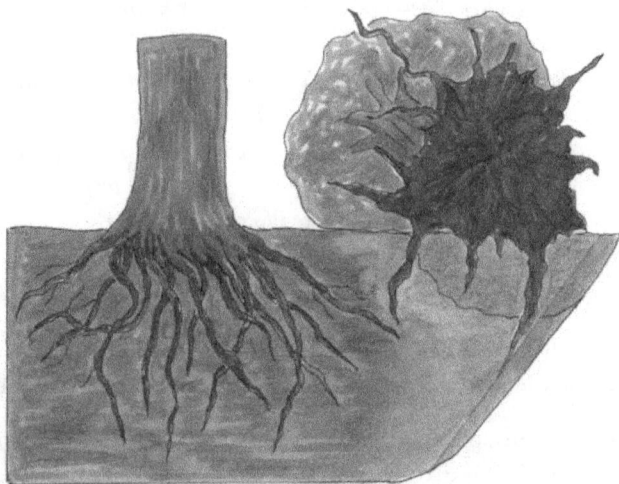

A tree with deep roots will not topple during a storm. A tree with shallow roots will quickly fall when the wind gets strong.

Science Facts: Understanding Nonlinear Phenomena in Nature

Nonlinearity, what is it? In nature we see all events take place through cause and effect. It is a basic principle that every outcome, every effect has a cause that led to the outcome. A 'linear' cause and effect is a process that is predictable by simple laws of physics. Each cause leads to simple effect. For example: heating water; Newton's laws of motion, etc. A 'nonlinear' cause and effect is when the cause leads to a change that multiplies the effect. The result can become bigger than expected and can get out of control. In addition, the effect becomes very difficult or impossible to predict.

Changes in weather patterns, starting from an initial cause, belong to the non-linear category. For example:

1. The Butterfly Effect: because of the complexity of the factors that control the weather, a very slight change of initial conditions leads to unpredictable results.

2. Explosion: when you mix two chemicals that react so fast that the outcome is an explosion, not just a small change.

Lessons from God's Two Books

Thomas Paine:

For lack of a nail the shoe was lost,
For lack of a shoe the horse was lost,
For lack of a horse the man was lost,
For lack of a man the battle was lost.

We learn that small habits can become big habits that become uncontrollable: like smoking, drugs, alcohol, stealing, complaining, ungratefulness. Some affect our physical bodies (drugs, etc.) and some affect our inner soul (ungratefulness, anger, etc.) Both types can become addictive and the longer you practice the habit the more addicted you become and the harder it is to quit.

- **Negative:** A small lie could lead to more and bigger lies to cover the truth.

- **Positive:** If you tell someone about life in Jesus Christ and he tells two other people and then the two others tell two others, before you know it, the whole school or city or country would hear about the wonderful good news that Jesus came to give us life

Fun with Science

Observe Natural Instabilities

Supplies:

- Tall glass
- Water
- Food Coloring

1. Fill the glass with water, let the water settle and become very still.
2. Gently place a couple of drops of food coloring on the surface of the water. Food coloring dye is heavier than the water, so it will sink. As it sinks it should form a small ring, which separates into smaller rings, which then separate into even smaller rings. Instability within the rings causes them to break up into smaller rings, and this should continue until the bottom is reached or dye is diluted.

This is a simple illustration of complex fluid motions. The experiment is easy, but the instabilities produced are very hard to model mathematically. This is an example of the Rayleigh-Taylor Instability: **an instability of an interface between two fluids of different densities, which occurs when the lighter fluid is pushing the heavier fluid** (Sharp, D.H. (1984). "An Overview of Rayleigh-Taylor Instability." Physica D 12: 3–18).

174

Create a Storm Bottle

Supplies:

- Empty water bottles
- Water
- Oil (vegetable oil is fine)
- Food Coloring

1. Fill the bottle approximately 1/3 full with vegetable oil.

2. Fill the rest with water (but don't overflow).

   Note that the molecules of oil and water do not mix—when you pour water into oil, the water sinks to the bottom (why do you think this occurs?). Even if you shake the bottle the oil breaks into small droplets that do not mix with water.

3. Add about 10 drops of food coloring (make it any color you want—but you can use blue to mimic the ocean).

   Notice that the food coloring only mixes with the water—it does not color the oil.

4. Screw on the bottle cap, turn the bottle on its side, and tip the bottle gently back and forth to watch the wave appear.

   Waves are just energy moving through water. If you hold a jump rope at both ends and create a wave, you will see that the wave moves but the jump rope only moves up and down, but not forward. Similarly, the water of the wave itself doesn't move, it's the energy passing from one water molecule to another that forms the waves. Ocean waves are caused by several things such as wind, pull from the moon's gravity, the way the ocean floor is shaped, and the spinning of Earth on its axis. Waves crashing on the beach are caused by the bottom of the wave dragging on the shallow shore while the top keeps going. This causes the curl (also known as the break) in the wave.

Other activities to study Weather and Wave Motion

1. Try the Jump rope demonstration—look at waves traveling along a fixed line.
2. Domino Effect (or use a deck of cards to do the experiment).
3. Hearsay illustrates the nonlinear effect of communication.
4. Mixing two chemicals resulting in an explosive mix
5. Linear effect: the amazing effect of factorials

Order in Disorder

✓ Flip a coin and drop a coin (statistical vs. determined)
✓ The **Sierpinski Triangle** is a fascinating example of order in disorder or the relationship between random actions (chaos) and order. Begin by marking three points to form the three points of a triangle. Then put your pen anywhere within the perimeter of the triangle (random process). This will be your 'current position.' From your 'current position' make another point halfway between it (ordered process) and one of the vertex points. Again, from this new 'current position' make a point halfway between it and another vertex point. Continue to do this, randomly picking points between your 'current position' and one of the vertex points, a hundred thousand times. This process is an interplay between a random choice and a specific rule, that of the halfway mark. Of course, you do not have time to do this, but a computer can do it quickly. What emerges is an ordered diagram (also called fractal) that contains triangles within triangles within triangles. This is a great example of how order emerges out of chaos, or random choices.

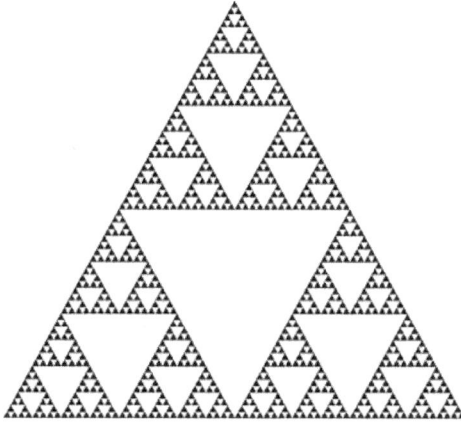

You can see the process actually take place. A computer-generated
Sierpinski Triangle can be seen at the following site: http://
en.wikipedia.org/wiki/sierpinski_triangle
Or go to Wikimedia and search for the Sierpinski Triangle

Recently, studies in biochemistry that have to do with organisms
like antibodies that make up our immune system, show that these
antibodies (molecules or organisms) are generated completely by
random processes initiated by our genes on the DNA code.

Staying in Touch: Prayer

One day Jesus was praying in a certain place. When he finished, one of his disciples said, "Master, teach us to pray just as John taught his disciples." So he said, "When you pray, say,   Father,
Reveal who you are.   Set the world right.
Keep us alive with three square meals.
Keep us forgiven with you and forgiving others.
Keep us safe from ourselves and the Devil."

Then he said, "Imagine what would happen if you went to a friend in the middle of the night and said, 'Friend, lend me three loaves of bread. An old friend traveling through just showed up, and I don't have a thing on hand.'

"The friend answers from his bed, 'Don't bother me. The door's locked; my children are all down for the night; I can't get up to give you anything.'

"But let me tell you, even if he won't get up because he's a friend, if you stand your ground, knocking and waking all the neighbors, he'll finally get up and get you whatever you need.

"Here's what I'm saying: Ask and you'll get;   Seek and you'll find; Knock and the door will open."

(Luke 11:2-4, The Message; see also Matthew 6:9-13)

Ask   Seek   Knock

Why is it important to pray? What difference does prayer make? Is God reluctant to answer our prayers, like the man Jesus speaks of, who was in bed already and didn't want to get up when his neighbor asked for bread? Is prayer just repeating a formula or performing a ritual in order to please God?

A story is told of the famous scientist, James Clerk Maxwell, who was a believer in Jesus Christ. He often spent time in prayer and meditation. As a result, he wondered how it was possible for God to perform actions at a distance, and to answer prayers from someone on earth. This may have influenced his eventual development of the Electromagnetic Theory. His initial equations appeared in 1861 in a paper entitled, *On Physical Lines of Force.* Electromagnetic Theory explains how invisible waves propagate (spread) across space.

God has the power to do everything himself. However, he has chosen to work in partnership with his creatures—you and me. Prayer starts with an understanding of who God is and what he wants to do. That is what the first two sentences of the Lord's Prayer are about. In prayer we can be honest before God, our Father, and tell him our needs and desires. (Keep us alive with three square meals.) Confession and forgiveness keep our line of communication open with God, because if we allow sin to build up in our lives, it separates us from God and makes it difficult for God to answer our prayers (Isaiah 59:1, 2). If we really understand how amazing God's forgiveness is, then we will be quick to forgive others. Forgiving others is an outward sign of our inward acceptance of God's forgiveness.

Finally, in prayer we ask for protection from evil. We live in an evil world and Satan is always trying to get us off track. Sometimes he directly tempts us, and other times we allow ourselves to be tempted by following our own desires and putting ourselves first.

Think about what would happen if you were lost in the wilderness. First you would try to establish some landmarks like mountain tops or the direction of the setting sun. Then you would try to make contact with someone who could help. First you would probably use your cell phone, but what if it didn't work! You could make a fire and send up smoke, or write "HELP" in big letters using dirt or trees or cloth. Finally, you need to keep alert for danger, either from wild animals or natural phenomena like lightening or other people who could harm you. This illustration gives you an example of why prayer is important. First we need to establish where we are, then ask for help, and finally be alert for danger. The Lord's Prayer summarizes this beautifully.

God is not reluctant to answer our prayers. In fact, Jesus says to ask and seek and knock. He wants us to come honestly and boldly before God the Father in prayer. However, the effectiveness of our prayers will depend on our understanding of who God is and what His Kingdom is about. That is why we start our prayer with, "Our Father, reveal who you are and set the world right (thy kingdom come, thy will be done on earth as it is in heaven)."

Science Facts: Understanding Telecommunications

Telecommunication means sending and receiving messages over long distances using radio waves or microwaves such as TV, radar, telephone or satellites. Radio waves or microwaves are part of the Electromagnetic (EM) spectrum which we discussed in Section 1, chapter 7. Wavelengths range from 100 meters down to 0.001 meter (1-40 gigahertz frequency). These very small waves, called microwaves, transmit conversation, music, pictures or data invisibly through the air or in a vacuum over distances exceeding millions of miles.

Radio waves and microwaves are generated using electronic devices. They are then transmitted by antennas which convert the electrical signal to EM waves. The best way to generate radio waves (or microwaves) is by using a circuit that consists of a capacitor and an induction coil. By choosing the right components, you can select the frequency (or wavelength) you will be generating. In order to have the radio waves transmit a message, the transmission needs to be modulated, which means that the frequency, amplitude or phase of the wave needs to be adjusted. The two most common types of modulation used in radios are amplitude modulation (AM) and frequency modulation (FM). Examples of both of these modulations can be seen below.

Optional: a more detailed explanation of radio frequencies:

Receiving antennas intercept part of this radiation and change it back to a form of electrical signal and feed it to a receiver. The superheterodyne (picture on right) is the most common circuit for radio-frequency selection and amplification used in radio receivers. Incoming signals are mixed with a signal from a local oscillator to produce intermediate frequencies (IF) that are equal to the arithmetical sum and difference of the incoming and local frequencies. One of those frequencies is applied to an amplifier. Because the IF amplifier operates at a single frequency, namely the intermediate frequency, it can be built for optimum selectivity and gain. The tuning control on a radio

receiver adjusts to the local oscillator frequency. If the incoming signals are above the threshold of sensitivity of the receiver and if the receiver is tuned to the frequency of the signal, it will amplify the signal and feed it to circuits that demodulate it (separate the signal wave itself from the carrier wave).

Microwaves are also used to transmit power such as that used in microwave ovens or radar. Microwave power is generated by means of a magnetron or a klystron. In a klystron an electron gun produces a flow of electrons that are 'bunched' into a cavity. A 'bunching' cavity then regulates the speed of the electrons so they arrive in the bunches at the output cavity. The bunches of electrons excite the microwaves in the output cavity of the klystron. The microwaves flow into a waveguide, which modulates and transports them to an antenna. The simplest analogy that can help us understand a klystron and how it converts electric power to microwaves is the example of an organ pipe. Blowing into the organ pipe produces a flow of air. Flowing air excites vibrations in the cavity of the whistle or pipe. The vibrations flow into the surrounding air as sound waves which our ear drums pick up and, through the intricate process of the inner ear, are translated to our brains as music.

Illustration of Amplitude Modulation:

Note that the frequency (length between waves) is the same, but the height (amplitude) of the waves differ.

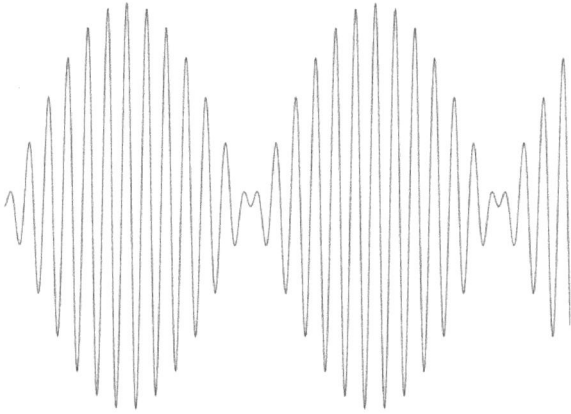

Illustration of Frequency Modulation:

Note that the height (amplitude) of each wave is the same, while the frequency (length between waves) differs.

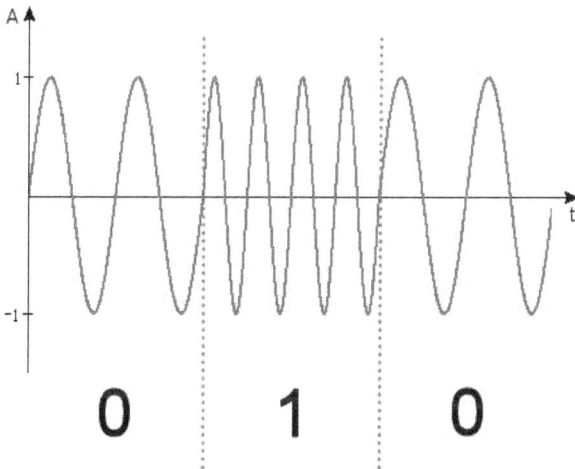

Fun with Science

Let's make a radio and pick up the radio waves that are all around us.

- www.sci-toys.com (steps to make a radio using stuff you have around the house)

- www.electronickits.com (radio-making kits)

- Snap Circuits: easy to handle, fun electronic kits available from many retailers.

Doing My Best

"Whatever you do, whether in word or deed,
do it all in the name of the Lord Jesus."

Colossians 3:17

The people featured in Bible stories are often people with many faults. The fact that the Bible does not sugarcoat their lives, making them into 'holier than thou' characters, adds to the authenticity of the stories. However, Daniel is presented as a man with few faults. Daniel is an example of a life well lived, faithful to both his God and to his sovereign. The amazing thing about this is that the sovereign was not a good king, or even a Jewish king, but an evil, pagan king who worshipped idols. Daniel shows us how to live in an evil world with wisdom, able to discern the difference between principles (those beliefs that are unchangeable) and preferences (those behaviors that are culturally learned).

Daniel was captured as a young man by the Babylonians, the powerful and merciless enemies of his home country, Israel. He saw his country destroyed, and possibly his family also. He was taken as a slave to a foreign land where Jehovah God was not honored. These circumstances would cause most people to give up their faith and hope, and seek to just survive. But as we learn in the book of Daniel, his faith did not waver but in fact grew stronger. He knew when to 'draw the line' between what pagan practices he would participate in and what practices he would refuse. It is interesting that he chose to take the pagan name, Belteshazzar (*"May Bel Protect His Life"*) given him and learned the skills and knowledge of pagan teaching. But he refused to eat food that had been offered to pagan idols. He did not simply refuse, but came up with a creative solution, asking the steward to do an experiment. The test was to see if by eating vegetables only, Daniel and his fellow prisoners would remain as healthy as if they had eaten all the 'goodies' from the king's table. They ended up being even more healthy than those who ate from the kings table and so were allowed to keep eating vegetables, avoiding the food that had been offered to idols.

Daniel was a man of prayer. He prayed faithfully three times a day and continued even when jealous men spied on him, trying to turn the king's heart against him. Daniel was not afraid and knew how to stand alone. When these men tried to find something against him in order to get him fired, they could find nothing. Daniel was a man of unimpeachable character. He did his job so well that he continued to serve a succession of three kings—two Babylonian and one from among the Medes and Persians. He became indispensable!

He was also well-liked by the kings because he carried no spirit of bitterness, in spite of the things that happened to him. He did not consider himself a 'victim' but a representative of Jehovah God in the court of a pagan king. He respected the authority he had been put under and knew how to approach that authority in diplomatic ways (Daniel 2:14) and with creative solutions. In the end, the kings gave glory to his God because of Daniel's testimony. (Nebuchadnezzar in Daniel

4:34-35; Belshazzar in Daniel 5:13-14; Darius in Daniel 6:25-27).

For these reasons, Daniel is a wonderful example of a young man who 'did his best' in a difficult and challenging situation. His Hebrew name, Daniel, means 'God is my judge.' He was a man of wisdom and brought glory to God by his actions, words and life because he lived out his name, recognizing that *"the fear of the Lord is the beginning of wisdom."*

Robert Boyle (1627-1691)

An example of a man who lived an exemplary Christian life and excelled in his scientific endeavors

Robert Boyle or "Robin" as he was called, was the 14th child of the second wife of Richard Boyle, the first Earl of Cork. The Boyle home was nominally Christian but in fact, Richard Boyle sought position, power and material gain more than God. Robin had the chance to learn much from his older brothers and sisters, and by the time he was a young man, realized that life was serious and he must make a choice between worldly ways and God's ways. As a child he woke up one night to a powerful electrical storm engulfing his home. His fear reminded him of the fear of meeting the Almighty God someday and he vowed to commit his life to God and to obey His Word.

From that day forward, Robert Boyle kept his vow to a remarkable degree. He was very intelligent and often had doubts about his faith, but instead of turning away, he sought the answers even more diligently and became a well-known apologist for the Christian faith. He learned Greek so that he could read the New Testament in the original language. He wrote, "He whose Faith never doubted, may justly doubt of his Faith." Boyle never lost his 'Fear of the Lord' and his respect for the Creator God. He gave generously to help the poor and supported a number of Bible translation projects. He believed in the dignity of each person no matter their position and when debating someone with whom he disagreed, he never resorted to name-calling or degrading comments. In the same spirit, he hated divisions among Christian brothers and worked diligently to promote a gracious and gentle spirit among those who followed the various, often differing, Christian doctrines.

Beginning at age twenty-three, Boyle developed a life-long passion for experimental science. Modern scientific investigation was just beginning to develop. Until this time, scientific inquiry had been influenced by Aristotelian thinking that regarded 'Nature' as semi-divine and able to 'work miracles.' This belief limited the free investigation of cause and effect. Boyle strongly supported the position that one should not use divine omnipotence (power) to explain natural phenomena. In 1663, he was one of the founders of the Royal Society of London for the Improvement of Natural Knowledge and made major contributions in understanding the relationship between air and sound, the expansion of freezing water, specific gravity, and also in crystals, electricity, color and hydrostatics. Chemistry was his favored field, however, and his most famous contribution is Boyle's Law. This law states that in closed space, when the pressure (P) on a gas increases, its volume (V) decreases in direct proportion at any given temperature.

Today we still benefit from another one of Boyle's

contributions—the barometer. In 1645 Toricelli was the first to design an instrument for measuring air pressure. Boyle made improvements on this design and ten years later gave it the name 'barometer', which means 'weight measurer.' It was an important tool for Boyle's numerous experiments attempting to weigh and measure air. Its use in weather forecasting came much later through the efforts of Robert Fitzroy in 1850-1860.

Boyle promoted science that focused on mechanical means (cause and effect) and not immaterial (nature or god) agents. His approach became known as 'Mechanical Philosophy.' His work and thought were very instrumental in moving the study of matter from 'alchemy' to 'chemistry' and for that reason he is considered one of the founders of modern chemistry. Alchemy invoked 'mysterious forces' such as witchcraft in altering materials, whereas Boyle's mechanistic studies simply studied the facts of causes and effects. He felt that this in no way diminished one's wonder or worship of God, but, in fact, enhanced it because people would be even more astonished at the wisdom and purpose God had put into his creation and the consistency and intelligence of the laws he created. Jeremiah 31:35 uses the same approach to impress the omnipotence of God upon its hearers. *"This is what the Lord says, he who appoints the sun to shine by day and decrees the moon and stars to shine by night, who stirs up the sea so that its waves roar—the Lord Almighty is his name."*

Boyle was a strong advocate of God as the Designer and believed that worship is enhanced when the object of worship is a God of intelligence and order, as opposed to a God who does mysterious things in nature that we can't explain. By understanding the amazing intricacies of our world around us, he believed that, "Men may be brought, upon the same account, both to acknowledge God, to admire Him, and to thank Him." He even wrote of God's "3 Volumes, The Booke of Nature, the Book call'd Scripture, and the Booke of Conscience." Robert

Boyle sought throughout his life to examine, understand and live according to God's Books, which makes him an outstanding example and role model for Christians today, especially those who pursue the study of nature through modern scientific inquiry.

Science Fun: Boyle's Law

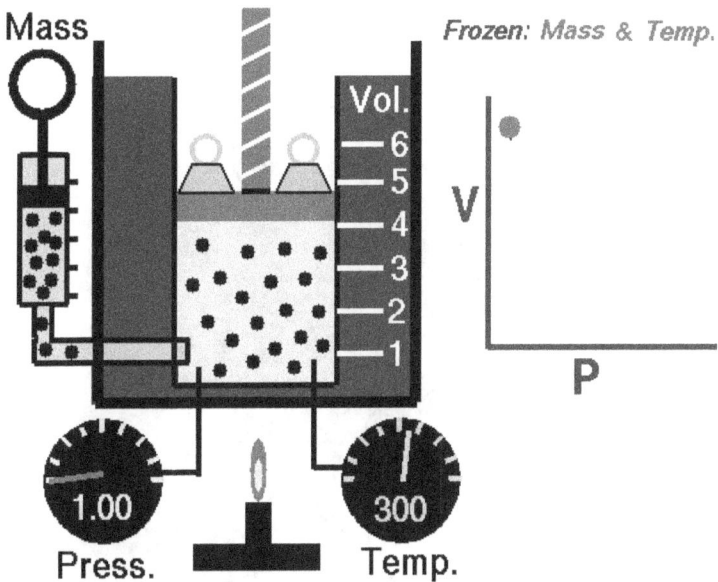

Boyle's Law states that in closed space, when the pressure (P) on a gas increases, its volume (V) decreases in direct proportion.

For Boyle's Law to work, the temperature is held constant. A further extension of his formula is to add temperature T as a third variable, along with V and P, thus:

$$\frac{P_1V_1}{T_1} = \frac{P_2V_2}{T_2}$$

Robert Boyle, although a Christian believer, worked to keep science separated from faith-based explanations. He is known as a Father of Modern Chemistry, because he helped change alchemy to chemistry.

"I THINK YOU SHOULD BE MORE EXPLICIT HERE IN STEP TWO."

References

1. Freeman Dyson, Institute of Advanced Studies, Princeton, N.J., Sci. News, August 24, 1974

2. Edward Witten, *The Man Who Led the Second Superstring Revolution*, Discover Magazine, 13, Nov. 2008

3. Martin Vetman, *Facts and Mysteries in Elementary Particle Physics*, World Scientific Publication, 2003

4. Hugh Ross, *Beyond the Cosmos*, NavPress, 1996, ch. 8

5. Kenell Touryan, *A Cord of Multiple Strands,* Appendix 2.

6. *Teaching Science in a Climate of Controversy: A view from the American Scientific Affiliation*, 1986.

7. Sir Mortimer Adler, *Ten Philosophical Mistakes,* MacMillan, NY & London, 1985.

8. *Science*, Vol. 325, 25 Sept. 2009, pg. 1629-1630.

9. *American Physical Society News*, June 1999 & October 1999, APS Approved Definition of Science

10. Josh McDowell, *New Evidence that Demands a Verdict*, Nelson Reference, Rev. Upd edition, Nov. 1999, ch 3.

Index

WONDERS IN OUR WORLD